last words

last words
CONSIDERING CONTEMPORARY CINEMA

JASON WOOD

WALLFLOWER PRESS
LONDON & NEW YORK

A Wallflower Press Book
Published by
Columbia University Press
Publishers Since 1893
New York • Chichester, West Sussex
cup.columbia.edu

Copyright © Jason Wood 2014
All rights reserved.
Wallflower Press® is a registered trademark of Columbia University Press

A complete CIP record is available from the Library of Congress

ISBN 978-0-231-17196-0 (cloth)
ISBN 978-0-231-17197-7 (pbk.)
ISBN 978-0-231-85069-8 (e-book)

Contents

Acknowledgments vii
Preface by Andrew Kötting ix
Introduction 1

Lenny **Abrahamson** 5
Clio **Barnard** 11
Marco **Bellocchio** 15
Anton **Corbijn** 20
Florian **Henkel von Donnersmarck** 25
Fernando **Eimbcke** 31
Michel **Gondry** 36
Joanna **Hogg** 41
Tom **Kalin** 49
Charlie **Kaufman** 56
Gideon **Koppel** 60
Harmony **Korine** 66
Andrew **Kötting** 72
Joe **Lawlor** and Christine **Molloy** 76
Ray **Lawrence** 85
James **Marsh** 91

Christopher **Nolan** 100
Christian **Petzold** 104
Nicolas **Winding Refn** 108
Kelly **Reichardt** 112
Ben **Rivers** 116
Ira **Sachs** 123
Celine **Sciamma** 128
Peter **Strickland** 132
Tilda **Swinton** 140
Wim **Wenders** 146
Ben **Wheatley** 151
Michael **Winterbottom** 155

Acknowledgments

My sincere gratitude to Yoram Allon at Wallflower Press, Curzon Cinemas, Jake Garriock, Andrew Kötting, Chris Petit, Ana Santos, Ian Haydn Smith and all of the filmmakers included in this book.

Dedicated to the memory of Artificial Eye co-founder Andi Engel who understood that film is an industry, but also an art. And vice versa.

This book is also dedicated to the memory of Walter Wood.

FORE **WORDS**
by Andrew Kötting

> The more injured you are by time – the more you seek to escape it – to write a faultless page – or only a sentence – it raises you above becoming and its corruptions – and you transcend death by the pursuit of the indestructible in speech – in the very symbol of nullity.
>
> **E.M. CIORAN – *THE TROUBLE WITH BEING BORN***

In This World
The Old Kent Road had a hold of me – motorbike on top of me – someone had driven into me – the blood spilled out from the femoral artery – I felt a warm oilglow piss all over me – I hadn't long in this world – me and my biography – *Lookatme* and *Woeisme* – I was awash and still it came gushing out – then a policewoman tiptoed through the mire to help me – she pushed hard into me – a gore-soaked poultice – 63 stitches – picture that – picture this – picture the puss – pictures – the story begins thus

My grandfather Albert (Gladys's husband) took me to the pictures – *Enter the Dragon* – *Bring Me the Head of Alfredo Garcia* – He told me that pictures could be dangerous – (he'd once found a photograph of somebody with their legs blown off up a tree) – but he didn't frighten me – *Hold the whole world up in front of a mirror for us all to see* – this was my philosophy – but real life had fallen into the cracks between myself and my work and caused much misery – deliriously – *The trouble with being born*

So
Ever onwards – forewards – an introduction as opposed to an outroduction – a reflection and pontification upon the main **stream (of consciousness)** – and all

this from *the moon that dreamed like an elephant's piss* – (post-accident morphine haze) – and into the unchartered pondwater of befuddled misremembrances – McQueen with his falling house and epic eye for detail – McQueen and the sexy train scene now followed by TS Eliot's agonies:

> Or as, when an underground train, in the tube
> Stops too long between stations
> And the conversation rises and slowly fades to silence
> And you see behind every face the mental emptiness deepen
> Leaving only the growing terror of nothing to think about.

The *shoutingout* and melancholy of the nothing-but-the-body – Carol Ann Duffy with her mirror in **I Remember Me** – *It must be dreams that make us different – must be the private cells inside a common skull* – The same but different – The shouting-out and melancholy of the *nothingbuthebody* – the same but different – **Main Stream** as the common current through which thoughts of the masses might easily flow – clones and echo chambers – pale imitations of themselves and real life – compromised committees – bandwagoneering not pioneering – universal not personal – the production of film not the medium of film – long-in-the-tooth and eversotired – straight from the board's mouth – devolved to the lowest common denominator – vanilla not rum and raisin

Sad

One can be sad anywhere but sadness grows in intensity within the confines of closed spaces – within the confines of a cinema that keeps showing the same faces – again and again and again – melancholy flourishes in open spaces – melancholy is fire-in-the-belly – is Nick Cave and Ned Kelly – Get out there and look for it – Not as business interest or capital venture but more an attempt at *punctum* – more an attempt at trying to make meaningful that which is meaningless – Gideon Koppel and his sheep – Clio Barnard and her ability to make you weep – the world closing in as real outburst and controlled angst – it can get lonely – Not Octavio Paz *Labyrinth of Solitude* lonely – more a really out there lonely – wind in the face tears in the eyes lonely – isolation and outsiderdom fuels and inspires – allows for a reflection – distance causes desire

The Industry

Of Film filling the horizon – fetid stream of settledown – gulag and fish farm – the major studios drying their nets in the Nissan huts of comic-book ambition – (another issue being the risk of algal blooms from overcrowding) Big Fish in One-Big-Pond – oxygen depletion and idea starvation – blocking out the sun and polluting the head – Who would ever want to penetrate the perimeter fence in order to swim in such fishy waters? Why dine at the table of plentitude when there are plenty of berries in the forest? Genre is a minimum-security prison in which all the guards are reading *Hello* magazine – contingent or specialised is elsewhere – An Edgeland where it might be possible to dive headlong into the *notknowing* – Christine Molloy and Joe Lawlor have been there – Harmony Korine lives there

Outside In
Really out there – Not In and pretending to be Out – *Contingency Solidarity and Irony* – The struggle between pragmatism and poetry – between philosophy and high energy – This is what Richard Rorty and Tarkovsky have taught me – Or De Montaigne – (Prophet of the Enlightenment) A mind unable to sit still – Explorer of the great themes of existence – humanist skeptic and acute observer – Georges Perec – *A Void* and *Life a User's Manual* – Lives seen through the prism of one's own self-consciousness – intrigue me astound me – do more than entertain me – disrupt the very fabric of the life that surrounds me – cut holes in it and let the light shine in

Maybe I should start again?

> When people talk about Modern Art they usually think of a type of art which has completely broken with the traditions of the past and tries to do things no artist would have dreamed of before. Some like the idea of progress and believe that art too must keep in step with the times. Others prefer the slogan the-good-old-days and think that modern art is all wrong.
>
> **E.H. GOMBRICH – *THE HISTORY OF ART***

Why do you have to be a non-conformist like everybody else?
Beyond the turmoil and effervescence of the busy life a quieter existence enjoys the surrounding splendor – in all its exquisite detail – Ben Rivers has supped from this forest floor and regurgitated atop the veneer banqueting table of superficial pop – Calm through the absence of cacophony and CGI – an essential antidote to the business of mediocrity and commerciality – James Marsh and Anton Corbijn – mirrors of the mainstream but with more spit and less furniture polish

> And you are not paying for art. You are paying for assurance, for social confirmation of your investment, and the consequent mitigation of risk. You are paying to be sure, and your assurance is very expensive, because risk is everything, for everybody, in the domain of art.
>
> **DAVID HICKEY – *AIR GUITAR***

The peloton of commercial success
And all those films that you hear far too much about – shining examples of perfected advertising – propaganda and manipulating – riding roughshod over embryonic Jarmans Framptons and Potters – old school breakaway groups – pockets fairly full to overflowing with the not-knowing and the questing – we are enriched only by frequenting disciplines remote from our own

Risk
So all risks are modeled on those that have gone before – the cakes might look different but the ingredients are the same – the butchers the bakers and the candlestick makers all setting up stall in the matching market square – where is the precarious instability and awkward vulnerability? Tilda Swinton, Peter Strickland and Ben Wheatley – come show me

Alternative
Error as a celebration and distortion of truth – and these works are erroneous because they drink from the trough of marginal truth – they re-present themselves as regurgitated half truths – exhilarating and roughly hewn stabs of new happinesses

> *It is important to acknowledge the instability of truth when making a film based on fact*
>
> **CLIO BARNARD**

> *You can't leave your brain at home on the sofa; you need to bring it with you to this cinema*
>
> **LIAM CUNNINGHAM – FATHER DOMINIC MORAN –** *HUNGER*

The sometimes
Sometimes lost – sometimes beached – sometimes abandoned – sometimes felt – sometimes known – sometimes wrong – sometimes lacking – sometimes needful – sometimes stunning – always questioning

> *There are no answers and there are not even any proper questions*
>
> **IAIN SINCLAIR – SWIMMING TO HEAVEN**

So
I leave you optimistic – the eternal quest – voyage without End – kicking against the pricks – needful of something to fight against but never alone – ongoing

PS

I happened upon this implied narrative yesterday on the way home from work. Culled from the side of the road in the form of a tumbledown neon sign:
COURTYARD AVAILABLE FOR SMOKERS AND NATURISTS

Meaning through free association

Because of David Shields, Iain Sinclair and Jason Wood

ANDREW KÖTTING, HASTINGS OLD TOWN, JULY 2013

Andrew Kötting was born in Elmstead Woods, England and went on to become a lumberjack in Scandinavia. Later, as an artist he trained at the Slade School of Fine Art in London, specialising in performance and film. He directed several experimental shorts that were awarded prizes at numerous international film festivals. *Gallivant* (1996), his debut feature film, is a seminal travelogue about his three-month journey around the coast of Britain with his grandmother Gladys and his daughter Eden.

In 2001 he directed the first of his Landworks trilogy, *This Filthy Earth*, for Film 4 and in 2009 *Ivul* for Artificial Eye. He continues to work on multi-media art projects including *Mapping Perception*, *In The Wake of a Deadad* and *Louyre*. *This Our Still Life* premiered at the Venice International Film Festival in 2011.

His most recent work, *Swandown*, was made in collaboration with the writer Iain Sinclair and shown extensively in cinemas across the UK and as an installation at Dilston Grove in London. The film had its French premiere at the Cannes Film Festival and will be distributed in France by E. D. Distribution.

Most recently Andrew was commissioned to work with the photographer Anonymous Bosch on a series of pinhole photographs inside a cave on top of the Mountain of Fear in the French Pyrenees.

Introduction

Published interviews with filmmakers are increasingly becoming a thing of the past. In a media enthralled by the notion of stardom and dictated to by commerce it has become rare to read an extended interview with a filmmaker, unless that filmmaker has made a film featuring a star that is likely to go on and make a considerable amount of money at the box office. The world of film PR is now so rigorously patrolled that even many A-list filmmakers rarely grant one-on-one interviews and when they do they are shoehorned into a twenty- or thirty-minute window; a time constraint that hardly allows for a detailed consideration of the work.

Every now and again a British filmmaker will appear and deliver a film that generates both critical and commercial heat and will thus earn themselves and their film column inches. Tom Hooper was everywhere after the success of *The King's Speech* (2010) as was Sam Mendes after breathing yet more life into the bloated, anachronistic corpse of the James Bond franchise with *Skyfall* (2012). Veteran British auteur types such as Ken Loach and Mike Leigh are also figures whose films and histories can be considered to reasonably justify interview time. If there is a story attached to the production, a couple of plucky first timers may break through. Peter Strickland's *Katalin Varga* (2009) became the story of a film made on an inheritance cheque whilst Clio Barnard's exceptional *The Arbor* (2010) had a journalistic angle in its tactic of having actors sync the words of actual people. Both films were deserving of the attention they were given.

The majority of the interviews in this collection are with British filmmakers who may otherwise have their work and their sensibilities go under the radar. British directors also frequently find themselves corralled together in a kind of catch-all piece designed to give the impression of editorial support. The *Observer* recently ran a series of short interview pieces with directors including Richard

Ayoade, Clio Barnard, Amma Asante and Joanna Hogg ('British Film on the Crest of a Wave', Tom Lamont, *The Observer*, 15 September 2013) off the back of recent festivals at Toronto and Venice. Despite the fact that each of these filmmakers operate in a very different style they were all placed together in a 'the British are coming'-type piece in which it was clear that the writer of the article had seen few if any of the actual films in question.

The move towards the mainstream has become unstoppable. Recent franchise and other unashamedly populist titles such as *Kick-Ass* (2010), *Avengers Assemble* (2012), *Iron Man 3* (2013), *Star Trek Into Darkness* (2013) and *This is 40* (2013) were all given four- and five-star 'lead review' treatment even in broadsheet publications such as the *Guardian*, the nation's favoured critical barometer. The traditional art-house releases, which over the last decade have increased in number to saturation point, are forced to take their place amongst the pack with even a well-reviewed title relegated to fourth or fifth billing and a review, no matter how positive, that may run to little more than a paragraph.

Periodically, most commonly on a quiet week for Hollywood, a specialised or foreign-language film such as *I Wish* (2011), *Our Children* (2012), *Amour* (2012) or *In The Fog* (2012) may enjoy top billing but these instances must now be considered anomalies. In reality these specialised titles rely on reviews to attract audiences as they simply don't have the benefit of a considerable marketing and advertising budget to increase their profile and broaden their reach. Without editorial support, and critics invariably blame editorial policy for the recent downsizing of attention to 'niche' titles, they have little chance of finding an audience and could conceivably disappear from our screens and our collective psyches.

With diminished review space, non-mainstream and foreign-language directors have become all but invisible and it is rare indeed to read an interview with a filmmaker who could be considered in some way specialised, a generic term that could be taken to mean foreign-language or aesthetically or financially independent in some way. There are, of course, a number of directors who can command press attention by virtue of the fact that their films regularly win international prizes, achieve a certain amount of box office and generally enjoy a wide release outside of their native domestic territories. Figures such as Pedro Almodovar, Michael Haneke and more recent additions to the ranks including Michel Hazanavicius and Asghar Farhadi are, however, firmly in the minority.

With the exception of *Sight and Sound*, which at the time of writing carries an interview with Abbas Kiarostami, there is little space given over either to more niche or unheralded auteurs or newly emerging voices whose work displays quality or distinction. The publication cannot carry the torch alone and for reasons related to space or economy – though subsidised it also has to generate income and shift copies – often has to prune back the word count for a piece on a specialised title in favour of a more headline-grabbing act. The aforementioned July

2013 issue places an interview with Richard Linklater for *Before Midnight* (2013) front and centre whilst Kiarostami's *Like Someone In Love* (2012) has a more backseat view. Jonathan Romney, a regular contributor to the magazine and one of the most high-profile supporters of specialised film has just been let go by *The Independent on Sunday*, a move which follows Robbie Collin replacing Sukhdev Sandu at *The Telegraph*. It is utterly conceivable that in an age when everyone has a digital voice that many national newspapers will stop covering film entirely. More critic casualties are certain to follow.

The demise of *Vertigo* was a considerable blow to both artists' cinema and world and European filmmakers and there has been nothing in the UK to replace it. There is also, as far as I can see, little evidence to suggest that online publications are filling the chasm created by the problems facing the printed press. There is more a sense digital déjà-vu, a repetition of pieces that we have already consumed elsewhere.

All of which is, of course, an attempt to justify the existence of *Last Words*. A follow-up of sorts to my earlier collection, *Talking Movies: Contempoeary World Filmmakers in Interview* (2007) and thus possibly the least anticipated film publication ever. This book collects together interviews with filmmakers and are all culled from conversations that have been conducted without interference over numerous years as a film programmer and occasional journalist. Many of these pieces have not appeared elsewhere and many were conducted as on-stage post-screening discussions, perhaps the last refuge of the in-depth film director interview. My preference has always been for film interviews to be published as transcripts to allow the filmmaker to communicate their ideas in an unfiltered form. The transcript is also a tactic for discounting the often-colossal ego of the interviewer and the supposition that readers are desperate to learn of the extent to which the interrogated and the interrogator got along. It is in transcript form that the interviews are presented to you here, with anything other than comments relating to the work itself judiciously removed.

The short introduction to each individual interview will hopefully indicate why I felt it was worth including (Christopher Nolan sticks out like a sore thumb but the interview was conducted pre-*Batman*), but in general this book is intended as a tool for people interested in cinema that occupies new or different territories. It also seeks to provide first-hand accounts of the filmmaking process from figures who could be considered to have a unique, challenging or non-conformist aesthetic vision. You may not have read these figures discussing their films in depth before and if the residual eradication of film culture continues in our press and on our screens there is a genuine danger that you may not hear their voices or opinions in the future.

Lenny **Abrahamson**

Lenny Abrahamson started shooting shorts while studying Philosophy at Trinity College, Dublin. After a period of post-graduate study in Philosophy at Stanford University in California, he returned home to concentrate on filmmaking.

Abrahamson's first two features were fruitful collaborations with writer Mark O'Halloran. The first, *Adam & Paul* (2004), was included in the Official Selection at the 2005 Berlin Film Festival. *Garage* (2007) was the recipient of the CICAE Art Cinema Prize in the Director's Fortnight at the 2007 Cannes Film Festival.

Featuring a truly remarkable performance from comic Pat Shortt as a mentally retarded attendant at a rural Irish petrol station, the *Garage* looks at the ultimately tragic turn his life takes when he tries to interact more decisively with society. It is characteristic of Abrahamson's work in its attentiveness to character and observations on the fragility of relationships.

Abrahamson's third feature is the recently released *What Richard Did* (2013), a quietly devastating tale set amongst a privileged set of South Dublin teenagers, through the summer between the end of school and the beginning of university.

The director is currently completing *Frank*, very loosely based on Frank Sidebottom and featuring Michael Fassbender.

The interview below took place on the eve of the release of *Garage*.

―――――

JASON WOOD: *Following the warmly received* Adam & Paul, Garage *marks your second consecutive feature collaboration with writer Mark O'Halloran. Could you talk about the working partnership and some of the sensibilities you share?*

LENNY ABRAHAMSON: Mark says that we plucked each other from obscurity and that's not far from the truth. There is a great connection between us artistically and a natural territory we inhabit when we work together. Looking at our films it's hard to disentangle his traces from mine. They are the result of real collaboration. Having said this, in terms of the way we work it's all quite traditional. We talk, he writes and I direct. Certainly this was true with *Garage*. On *Adam & Paul* everything was new and it took us a while to discover our method.

I think one of the big things that we share, which makes our collaboration possible, is that we don't like characters to be fully captured in a film. And we favour story over plot. What do I mean by this? Well, at the level of the characters, even though we create them, they are not reducible to a set of psychological traits or a list of motivations. And nor is it always easy for an audience to extract conventional plot points from the flow of events. Mark's writing is always open: the scenes feel true and are full of possible meanings; the voices are absolutely authentic. The scenes are somehow compelling but it would often be hard to say just why. That's the way life is: meaning is always there but there is no clearly given way of decoding it. Conventional cinema obscures this with an easy reduction of meaning to plot and schematic characters. Cinema at it's best can express something of the pure irreducible fact of things.

JW: *What advances do you see between* **Adam & Paul** *and your second feature, and what were the main lessons you learned?*

LA: I probably wouldn't use the word 'advances'. *Adam & Paul* is true to itself and complete and so for me is a fully realised piece of work. *Garage* is probably a deeper film, quieter, sparer, and more resonant. But that emerged through dealing with its content, not because we sat down after *Adam & Paul* and consciously decided to move in that direction. That's not to say I didn't learn from the first film. Shooting *Adam & Paul* was very tough. There was barely enough time and the budget was tiny. On top of that we shot in dangerous locations where we had little or no control or security. I was aware on *Garage* of defending a schedule that would give me space to work with more freedom. We also shot the film in a very beautiful, quiet place in the middle of the countryside. So the experience of making the two films was very different. Shooting *Garage* I felt relaxed, but at the same time intensely concentrated. I don't think I achieved the same purity of focus on the first film.

JW: *You have described* **Garage** *as 'slapstick tragedy' in that it brings together two genres that shouldn't necessarily match. What is it about marrying these two distinct genres that interests you as a filmmaker and were there specific pitfalls that you wished to avoid?*

LA: Probably this description better applies to the first film. *Adam & Paul* is more obviously Vaudevillian – it has lots more physical comedy as well some out and out slapstick routines in the 'who's-on-first' or Laurel and Hardy tradition. But there is still something of this in *Garage* in the way that elements of clowning are used. Josie is a kind of clown who's had most of his gags taken away from him and is left standing in the centre of the stage feeling dislocated and gormless. I find something moving about that style, without it ever being crudely emotive.

JW: *The perception of Josie changes as the film progresses. We begin with how he is perceived by others and journey towards a more internal and retrospective portrait. Apart from the performance of Pat Shorrt, what tactics did you employ to achieve this?*

LA: The film is always with Josie – it's a chronicle of his life over a number of months – and Pat's performance is so subtle and deep, and the film is open and quiet enough to let you watch him closely, that after a time it becomes impossible to sustain your first impression of the character. The beginning, which is deliberately straightforward and unremarkable in presentation, encourages the viewer to see Josie as harmless, idiotic, absurd and, above all, slight – but as the story develops this view of him becomes harder to hold on to.

There are scenes of him in nature, on his own at home, scenes with the horse, which open the film out and give it a denser texture and it becomes harder to think of Josie in easy social categories. Eventually as the film approaches the end sequence there is, I hope, a feeling that there is something unfathomable about him.

The important thing for me was to achieve this development without marking the changes in any obvious way. Josie could never describe his feelings – perhaps he is not even conscious that he has them. Actually, in a real sense, there is no change in Josie; no 'character development' to use that horrible phrase. The change is in us as we watch him. All his depth, all his capacity is there from the beginning – we just don't see it. The film works by becoming quieter, more concentrated as it moves forward, which draws the audience in and intensifies its awareness. In a way, everything points towards the few seconds of silent black screen after the last image and before the credits.

JW: *One of the things I most enjoyed about* **Garage** *is its willingness to communicate as much through what is left unsaid and suggested as that which is made explicit. For example, the scene where Josie makes tea for Mr. Gallagher and we are left in no doubt that Josie is about to lose his home and his livelihood. Was this approach a major decision for you?*

LA: We knew the scene you describe would end where it does, before anything significant is said. As shot it was longer, though – with all the dialogue you would expect – so that the actors could play the complete encounter and would not be anticipating the cut. Generally, there is an attempt in *Garage* not to load the dialogue with explicit meaning. I'm interested in the spaces between the significant moments in life, the parts that are usually discarded in memory and also – almost as a matter of principle – in conventional cinematic storytelling.

JW: *In terms of its visual characteristics, you employ a spare minimalist style. Is this partly informed by the natural beauty of your locations, and what other factors came into play when deciding the tact that you take?*

LA: The process of shooting of choosing shots is intuitive for me and I just feel my way towards what seems right. In fact, though the filmmaking is always quiet, there are places where the images are expressive as well as places where the shots are deliberately functional. It's hard for me to define a single visual style that describes the film. *Garage* is minimal, I suppose, in the sense of being as simple as I could possibly make it. When there really is something authentic in a scene, and when you remove everything that feels inflected in the storytelling, anything unnecessary, then the scene can acquire an extraordinary intensity. Lots of this business of taking things away happens in the edit. I try to take bricks out of the building, and as long as it doesn't fall down they stay out. The danger in making something like *Garage* where the events are mostly 'ordinary' – at least on the surface – in this very simple way is that if there is any kind of false note, then the powerfully prosaic becomes just prosaic. There is none of the bluster and effect of conventional drama to hide behind.

JW: *The minimalism is also reflected in the sparing use of music. Why did you decide to use so little?*

LA: I work with the same composer, Stephen Rennicks, on everything I do. I have a similarly tight relationship with him as I do with Mark. He's extremely talented and absolutely concentrated on his music as part of the film – never for its own sake. He composed beautiful, interesting music for many parts of the film and we would try pieces out, often keeping them in the cut for quite a while. But nearly always we came to feel that the sequence was stronger, purer, without the music. In the end there are three music cues left in the film; the titles and credits and one piece over picture. The music over titles is very dense, orchestrated and dramatic. It creates a kind of expectation that is undercut by the first, prosaic images of the film, but by the time a version of it recurs over the credits I think the expectation is met. The middle piece occurs at a very particular point in the film. It marks the end of something. Neither Stephen nor myself has ever worked as hard, or thought as much about film music as we did on *Garage*. There is so little of it but it is a hugely important part of the film.

JW: *There is a sense of timelessness with regards to the environment where the film is set. Given the ravages of modernity how difficult was it to find your location and what key elements – a garage presumably – were high on your list of priorities?*

LA: With the garage itself we were very lucky. The building that we ended up using – and using with almost no alteration – was due to be knocked down to make way for new apartments, just like in the story of the film. Generally though, and all breathless news reports about the Celtic Tiger notwithstanding, most of Ireland looks a lot like it always has. There were many, many towns we could have used. Strangely, one or two Irish critics have said that places like this no longer exist. I think they're watching too much TV.

JW: *Were there also certain images you were keen to avoid regarding the depiction of rural Ireland and smalltown life? In many ways you are not afraid to reveal that despite the beauty, there is a sense of frustration, boredom and even cruelty associated with this way of living.*

LA: I was concerned that while the film definitely had to show the insularity and occasional cruelty of smalltown life, it couldn't become about those things. There is a history of stage and film drama in Ireland – some of it wonderful – about the psychology of the depressed place, and for me there is not much to be said that's new. *Garage* is really a film about the significance of a small, unremarkable life and I wanted it to be a celebration of that life. It was often a difficult balance – to show it truthfully in all its sadness and at the same time to make it about something deeper than that sadness.

JW: *The relationship between Josie and David is beautifully realised before, of course, being tragically destroyed. How natural was the initially uneasy but then finally warm camaraderie we see between Pat and Conor?*

LA: Pat and Conor are easy going, open people and they liked each other from the beginning of rehearsals. Like David, Conor is self-possessed, gentle, and has a very developed, dry sense of humour. And he is as natural in front of the camera as any actor I've ever seen. Working with the two of them together was a great pleasure for me.

JW: *In a film of quietly remarkable performances – Anne-Marie Duff is especially striking – it is impossible not to come back to Pat Shorrt as Josie. I know that in Ireland he is a very popular comedian so did you have any reservations about casting him and how did you work together to achieve Josie's physical and mental appearance?*

LA: Once I thought about Pat as Josie it was impossible for me to imagine anyone else playing the part. We'd worked together briefly before and I knew that underneath his broad comedic style there was a great sensitivity as well as a profound understanding and familiarity with the kind of place Josie is from. If he had turned the part down – and I thought he probably would – I really don't know what we would have done. Pat is a performer, a character comedian, who is used to working from the outside in and that's a way that I like to work too. We didn't start with long conversations about Josie's feelings, or his history or his psychology. We started with how he walked, spoke, his bearing around other people, and we built him up that way, always with the script as our touchstone.

Certainly casting Pat in a straight role caused quite a stir in Ireland and at one point I remember I did worry the Irish audience would see only Pat and not Josie. But his performance is so extraordinary people very quickly forget they are watching Pat Shortt and become absorbed in the character.

Pat's performance still amazes me when I watch the film. I shaped the performance with him and I've seen it hundreds of times through the edit and at many screenings but I am still struck by how Pat, without any obvious 'acting', is able to give glimpses of Josie's deeper inner life. It is also striking how he can move seamlessly between almost high farce and a very dark, truthful, realistic performance.

JW: *The film, like* Adam & Paul, *was very warmly received and was relatively successful on its theatrical outing. Are you emboldened by its reception and has this in any way affected the scope with which you view your next project?*

LA: Yes, I am happy with how *Garage* has been received. It was by far the most successful Irish film of the year, which is saying something given the kind of piece it is. Its reception critically in other countries, particularly France and the UK, has also been extremely warm. This helps in getting the next projects funded and probably does open up possibilities for me to make bigger films. Having said that, I don't have any particular urge to make a bigger film for the sake of it. I like working on small films over which I have complete control. I'd hate to give up that freedom. There is one project I've been thinking about, though, which would have to be funded at a significantly higher level. Maybe it's now a real possibility that I could make that on my own terms. We'll see how it goes.

Clio **Barnard**

Clio Barnard's work deals with the relationship between documentary and fiction, and in particular the subjectivity of recollection. In 2006 Film and Video Umbrella commissioned Barnard to make *Dark Glass* as part of the *Single Shot* touring programme. A psychological micro-drama that moves from the sanctuary of a domestic garden to the half-remembered shadows of a house, the piece peers back into a semi-veiled interior world of fraught, ambivalent memories.

The tactic of constructing fictional images around verbatim audio (and vice versa) was brilliantly utilised in *The Arbor* (2010), Barnard's remarkable debut feature. Playwright Andrea Dunbar wrote unflinchingly about her upbringing on Bradford's Buttershaw Estate and was hailed as 'a genius straight from the slums' by playwright Shelagh Delaney. Dunbar's first play, *The Arbor*, originally written as part of a school assignment, described the experiences of a pregnant teenager with an abusive drunken father. Its success at the Royal Court Theatre led to Dunbar's commission to write *Rita Sue and Bob Too* in 1982. The play, and subsequent film by Alan Clark, was described as a portrait of 'Thatcher's Britain with its knickers down'.

Dunbar died tragically at the age of 29 in 1990, leaving her ten-year-old daughter Lorraine with bitter childhood memories. Having also grown up in the Bradford region, Barnard revisits the Buttershaw Estate to see how it had changed in the two decades since Dunbar's death and also catches up with Lorraine in the present day. Now aged 29, Lorraine is ostracised from her mother's family and in prison undergoing rehab. Re-introduced to her mother's plays and letters, the film follows Lorraine's personal journey as she reflects on her own life and begins to understand the struggles her mother faced. Through interviews with other members of the Dunbar family, we see a contrasting view of Andrea, in particular from Lorraine's younger sister Lisa, who idolises Andrea to this day.

Barnard recorded audio interviews with Lorraine Dunbar, other members of the Dunbar family and residents from the Buttershaw Estate over a period of two years. These interviews were edited to form an audio 'screenplay', which forms the basis of the film as actors lip-synch to the voices of the interviewees. This footage was intercut with extensive archive clips, as well as extracts from Andrea's stage play, filmed as a live outdoor performance on the Buttershaw Estate to an audience of its residents.

Transcending genre and defying categorisation, *The Arbor* emerges as a truly unique work, a celebration of Dunbar's triumphs and a dissection her legacy, both from a wider society perspective and on a personal level as we witness the pain of her short and tragic life.

Barnard has since completed *The Selfish Giant*, which premiered at the 2013 Cannes Film Festival to ecstatic notices.

JASON WOOD: *Your work has repeatedly demonstrated a concern with the relationship between fictional film language and documentary. How did you wish to engage with the subject of previous representations of the Buttershaw Estate on stage and screen and what was it about the techniques of verbatim theatre that struck you as being appropriate for* The Arbor*?*

CLIO BARNARD: Andrea's fiction was based on what she observed around her. She reminded the audience they were watching a play by her use of direct address when The Girl in *The Arbor* introduces each scene. I see the use of actors lip-synching as performing the same function, reminding the audience they are watching the re-telling of a true story.

My work is concerned with the relationship between fiction-film language and documentary. I often dislocate sound and image by constructing fictional images around verbatim audio. In this sense, my working methods have some similarity to the methods of verbatim theatre. Verbatim theatre by its very nature (being performed in a theatre by actors) acknowledges that it is constructed. Housing estates and the people who live there are usually represented on film in the tradition of Social Realism, a working method that aims to deny construct, aiming for naturalistic performances, an invisible crew and camera, adopting the aesthetic of Direct Cinema (a documentary movement) as a short hand for authenticity. I wanted to confront expectations about how a particular group of people are represented by subverting the form.

I used the technique in which actors lip-synch to the voices of interviewees to draw attention to the fact that documentary narratives are as constructed as fictional ones. I want the audience to think about the fact that the film has been shaped and edited by the filmmakers. Through these formal techniques I hoped the film would achieve a fine balance so that, perhaps paradoxically, the distancing techniques might create closeness, allowing a push/pull, so an audience might be aware of the shaping of the story but simultaneously able to engage emotionally.

Above all my hope is that the film will provoke compassionate thought and reflection.

JW: *You recorded audio interviews with Lorraine Dunbar and other members of the Dunbar family over a two-year period to create an audio screenplay. To what extent did you allow this audio screenplay to form the basis of the film and was it during this process that you decided to make Lorraine one of the central voices of the film, thus opening up the project into a consideration of inter-generational neglect as well as a dissection of Andrea's legacy?*

CB: The audio screenplay is the basis of the film and it was always the intention to do it this way round. I knew Lorraine was important because of her words at the end of *A State Affair* that linked back to Andrea's play *Rita Sue and Bob Too*.

At the point the film was commissioned I knew I wanted to speak to Lorraine because of these words but I didn't know what had happened to her in the ten years since. Neither did I know how autobiographical Andrea's play *The Arbor* was until I met her sister Pamela. Realising that the character of Yousaf in Andrea's play was Lorraine's father was key. Her play, combined with the interviews with her family, means that the film can look across three generations of a family and three decades of a particular place. I hope that this allows some understanding of the destructive effects of poverty, racism and addiction to emerge.

JW: *The lip-synching technique you employ in which your actors have to not only learn words but also master pauses and speech rhythms must have been very challenging. What casting process did you employ and how did you help the selected actors to cope with the rigors of the production?*

CB: I worked with a brilliant casting director called Amy Hubbard who brought in lots of actors who were up for the challenge. We asked them to try out the technique during the casting process. I have huge respect for the actors. It was very, very demanding on them. Manjinder Virk described it as being like learning a piece of music, and being like circular breathing. It meant that they had to be very present – never thinking ahead or they would trip up. The actors were incredible I think, and I'm indebted to them, not only for their remarkable technical skill but also for their ability to give true performances.

JW: *The approach that you take with the material and your concern over the boundaries between fact and fiction make for an incredibly immersive experience for the spectator. Did you wish to encourage an interpretative approach from the audience to what is on screen?*

CB: I wasn't totally certain what the effect of the lip-synching would be so it has been fascinating to learn about that from people who have seen it. People say that paradoxically the distancing technique draws them closer. I think it may be because all the people on screen look you in the eye. Perhaps you actively listen as a result.

JW: *I understand that* The Arbor *was not originally intended for cinema release. How did the positive critical reaction and the numerous prizes it has steadily accrued contribute to the film being allowed to find a wider audience than you perhaps originally intended?*

CB: It was commissioned by Artangel as a feature-length film for TV. The UK Film Council became involved during development and that was when it became intended for cinema release. Tracy O'Riordan, who is a brilliant producer, made certain that UK distributors saw the film as soon as it was finished. We were lucky that Verve picked it up. They have been great at getting the film out there, working alongside Rabbit PR; lovely, committed publicity people who made sure the critics saw the film. The response has been amazing and unexpected. I don't think you ever know how people are going to respond. I'm grateful to all the critics who were very open to and excited about the challenges of the film and to audiences for going to see the film and for their feedback.

JW: *Alongside recent works by Steve McQueen, Andrew Kötting, Joe Lawlor and Christine Molloy and Gillian Wearing,* The Arbor *highlights the continuing strength of artists' film in British cinema. Does this feel like an incredibly fertile period in which to be working?*

CB: I'm a great admirer of all these filmmakers. It is great that there hes recently been this strong strand of recent risk-taking British film, wonderful that these films are getting made and fantastic that they have found an audience. It's exciting to think that *The Arbor* is part of that.

Marco **Bellocchio**

Marco Bellocchio was born in Piacenza in 1939. In 1959 he left his Philosophy studies at the Cattolica University in Milan and enrolled at the Centro Sperimentale di Cinematografia in Rome. During 1961/62 he made the short films *Abbasso Lo Zio*, *La Colpa e La Pena* and *Ginepro Fatto Uomo* before moving to London to attend the Slade School of Fine Arts. Exploding onto the international film scene in 1965 with his fiery debut, *Fists in the Pocket*, Bellocchio is rightfully considered one of Italy's cinematic masters.

Vincere (2009) was the first Bellocchio film for some time to receive international distribution. The film tells a story airbrushed from many official biographies of Benito Mussolini; his relationship with Ida Dalser. A supporter of Mussolini from the time he was the ardent socialist editor of *Avanti!*, Dalser sells everything she owns to finance Mussolini's attempts to form the nucleus of what would become the Italian Fascist Party.

When the First World War erupts, Benito Mussolini enrols in the Army and disappears. When Dalser finds him again in a military hospital, he is tended to by another woman, who has just become his wife. Dalser lashes out at her rival, demanding her rights as Mussolini's true wife and the mother of his first-born son. She is led away by force. For more than eleven years, she is locked away in an insane asylum – and her son in an institute – where she is physically restrained and tortured, never seeing her son again.

―――

JASON WOOD: *What initially led you to the story of Ida Dalser?*

MARCO BELLOCCHIO: As an Italian I am familiar with the history of Fascism but the story of Ida Dalser was unknown to me. I discovered it through a documentary for Italian television. The documentary revealed that prior to becoming *Il Duce* in Milan before the war Mussolini had a love affair with a woman and they had a son. There is doubt over whether he actually married Ida but not that he recognised his son, Benito Albino. No official documentation of the marriage exists. What struck me following the broadcast of the documentary was the fact that everybody seemed to attribute a great deal of importance to the question of this marriage, as though the great tragedy of Ida lay in the fact that she had gone into a suicidal and self-destructive mode as a result of her abandonment. The fact of the marriage seemed to be of tremendous import to everybody. Even on the set of *Vincere* people would approach me and say 'Did they really get married?' That seemed to be of central importance, as opposed to the fact that Ida had abandoned herself to Mussolini and that she never relinquished this attachment. She refused to accept compromise, to the point of ending up in a mental asylum and the whole fate that then befell her.

JW: *The film reveals a great deal about Dalser's strength, her search to assert her own identity and her refusal to disappear despite the rejection and cruelty she suffers.*

MB: This wasn't necessarily my objective but it is nonetheless a clear characteristic of this woman. She was extremely tenacious and would not give even a millimetre on her iron will to re-conquer the man she had set her sights on. As Mussolini progressed in his political career, Ida found herself in an astonishing battle with him and by extension with the whole of Italy. Pitted against everybody; she had absolutely no support. Consequently this desperate fight of Ida's assumed a historic dimension. It also assumed a suicidal dimension. When the psychiatrist sees her at the hospital at San Clemente he suggests that Fascism will not last forever and therefore her absolute position of ferocious rebellion is self-destructive and self-defeating.

JW: *Although you have stated previously that you didn't wish for the film to serve as an exposition of the vileness of the Fascist regime, did you wish to interrogate the methods by which history represents, remembers and obscures?*

MB: It's a complex question. What the film does through private events and through the characters is offer a series of comments on historic memory. At a certain point Ida says to the psychiatrist, that if I don't do this, that is rebel, nobody will remember me. She wasn't wrong when she said this. In fact, it was by her extreme tenacity that she distinguished herself. Otherwise, had she not

Vincere, Marco Bellocchio, 2009 (Artificial Eye)

done that, she simply would have become one of the many women – and there were a great many in Mussolini's past – that were accepting of whatever position they were accorded.

I was interested in the events of a private person who was then completely squeezed out of historic memory. This person was denied the possibility of having any influence at all on Fascism or any other aspect of Italian history. My intention was not to tell the story of Italy, but any film or book will invariably allow some sort of image to emerge. What I was really interested in was depicting this tragedy, which is the tragedy of a mother and a son, using forms specific to that era. The use of the image was fascinating to me, hence the 'film within a film' aspect of *Vincere* and the various dialogues it has with images of Mussolini. The structure of the film incorporates an artificial Mussolini and a real Mussolini. You see images of Mussolini when he was young and then you see the real Mussolini as Ida and his son, Benito, saw him. I concentrated on the language of film in an attempt to tell this private story in combination with the history of Italy, or at least the photographic or filmic representation of the history of Italy and one of its key historical figures.

JW: *Was the decision to adopt this structure and incorporate the archive footage you refer to purely aesthetic?*

MB: When I was originally excited by the idea of this film I was also accepting of the fact that I clearly wasn't going to have anything like the means one would like to create it. As it happens, it was quite an expensive production – around 7 million Euros – but the form that it was going to take from the very outset was apparent to me and I was completely focused on this approach. My fascination with the interplay between image and representation was absolute, so thankfully my aesthetic approach was not constrained by my budget. The economics were always going to be incidental. To my mind simply recreating all the characters and events through fiction and performances only would have been unsatisfactory. Other films have adopted this approach, and not always successfully. One of the key elements to *Vincere* is the editing. We had to manipulate and appropriate the archive material to make it ours and to also personalise the story we intended to tell. Remember also that a lot of this material is already in the public domain and has been seen in countless documentaries. We did a lot of work on it, speeding it up, enlarging it, slowing it down etc in order to make it feel more personal and to enhance the interplay between the factual and fictive element of the film's structure. I think that even with 70 million Euros I would have avoided the temptation to simply recreate and film everything from new.

JW: *As well as the newsreel footage* Vincere *is also filled with numerous instances of film-watching: the wounded Mussolini watching a Biblical epic, Ida watching Chaplin.*

MB: This was a period of splendour for cinema. It had become hugely popular and attracted crowds in immense numbers. Until the advent of television cinemas were practically standing room only they were so crowded. The representation of these instances in the film is to show how there was this relationship with the outside world and these images. Ida does indeed watch a Chaplin film when she is in a mental asylum. She views it with the other inmates. When Mussolini is injured he begins to assume, in his own mind at least, the status of a martyr, identifying with the Christ figure, which is why I depict him watching the biblical movie. Using these moments from other films allowed me to underline certain points and parallels I wished to make. The popularity of cinema at this time, of course, also ensured that cinema could be used as an instrument. It was often the medium through which the individual and national consciousness – and indeed the sub-conscious – could be appealed to and modified.

JW: *Giovanni Mezzogiorno and Filippo Timi are striking in the central roles.*

MB: Timi was relatively easy to choose because he had such a strong physical resemblance to the young Mussolini. Timi also displayed a very natural authority. The role of Ida was much more complicated and we conducted a great many screen tests and looked at many actresses. We had to represent Ida at varying ages and even considered at a certain point casting two actresses; one to play the young Ida and one to play the older Ida. However, in the end Giovanni Mezzogiorno was somebody we found that had all the right qualities. She has a very beautiful face, but a face that also conveys great determination. Giovanni was also able to appear obstinate and sometimes unpleasant, though never sentimental, making her perfect for this part. I have to say that both Giovanni and Filippo were very generous in their commitment to their characters and in their desire to explore them. My role was mainly to modulate their performances, and to guide them.

JW: *It's apparent that you have a tremendous enthusiasm for the subject, but, and even after such a long and distinguished career, also for the medium.*

MB: There is a tendency for writers, filmmakers and other artists to repeat themselves or end up making work that could be considered banal. Without wishing to appear immodest my filmmaking career was initiated with the success of my debut, *Fists in the Pocket*, which gained international success. Because of this success I almost had to start all over again and so now, finding myself at a certain age, it is important to utilise all my knowledge and experience but also to only pursue subjects that I feel I can become completely involved in. Without sincerity and feeling for one's subject, this relative ambivalence will always be apparent in the result and in the images. Art doesn't allow for deception.

Anton **Corbijn**

Born the son of a Protestant minister in Strijen, Holland, Anton Corbijn began his career as a photographer. Moving to London in 1979 after establishing his work with the Dutch pop magazine *OOR*, Corbijn's photographs of the leading post-punk bands quickly established him as the photographer of choice for the *NME*. Joy Division, Depeche Mode and Captain Beefheart became three artists with whom Corbijn became closely associated.

Moving into the burgeoning music video field, Corbijn quickly mastered the medium and given his keen eye and affiliation with music it seemed a thoroughly natural progression when Corbijn turned his hand to feature-film directing with *Control* (2007). Partly based on the memoir *Touching From a Distance* by Ian Curtis's widow Deborah, the film's remarkable look at the life of Curtis and the band that he fronted is suffused with authenticity via Corbijn's affinity with the material and the northern backdrop from which the band emerged. Equally remarkable is the film's decision to view events from multiple perspectives.

Existential hitman drama *The American* (2010) is Corbijn's second feature. His third feature, *A Most Wanted Man*, will be released later this year.

―――――

JASON WOOD: *You were offered* Control *but originally passed as you didn't want your first feature to be a music film. Why did you change your mind?*

ANTON CORBIJN: I have always struggled with labels and for the first few years that I photographed I was correctly called a rock photographer but after that I had a problem with this label. I took a lot of photographs of musicians but I paid attention to the photography and not just who was in the photograph. Winding on a few years I began to try out various other visual disciplines, be it music videos or graphic and stage design. I had been reading scripts and really wanted to make a movie. Although some of the stories were good I never felt really comfortable enough to say, 'Okay. I'm going to make this film.' I had no education as a filmmaker and so I was convinced I would do it better than anybody else. I read the book that *Control* was based on and liked it very much but I was again concerned that it would be called a rock film and I would be cutting out quite a large audience. I think the film is far more universal than a biopic of Ian Curtis and Joy Division. For me it's a love story. Six months after declining I realised that it was such an important element in my life; after all, I had moved from Holland to England because of Joy Division, and so my incredibly emotional connection to the whole story convinced me that I could compensate for my lack of skills. I also began to think that this connection would allow me to do something with the film that perhaps somebody else would not be able to.

JW: *You announced the title before you made the film. What connotations does the title have for you?*

AC: It was just a working title initially but I didn't want to just call it *Touching From a Distance*, the title of the book by Ian's widow, because the film was about Ian and not about Debbie. I liked the way the title looked graphically and of course there is the obvious connection to the song, *She's Lost Control*. Ian was also a control freak and tried to control a lot of situations. He tried to control his marriage and he tried to control the band. You might not see this so much in the film. Of course there is also the epilepsy, a part of his life over which he had no control.

JW: *You reference Deborah's book but the film offers a variety of perspectives about Ian Curtis, including that of Annik Honore, who previously was poorly portrayed in the press.*

AC: I think it was important to show this. Annik was not a groupie. She was a girl that Ian fell in love with. For Ian, living in Macclesfield, she must have seemed very exotic. Knowing them both I can attest that they are very different women. I wanted to be neutral in the film, and of course Debbie's book is written entirely from her perspective. For the film I wanted to take Annik's situation into account. I read all of the letters that Ian wrote to her and it was obvious that he was very in love with her. Their relationship was driven by him and not by her and I don't think this has ever been clear before.

JW: *Samantha Morton is terrific. She does have a bit of a fearsome reputation.*

AC: I had met her before and she was actually the first person I had approached for the film. I worked with her a few years ago actually for a video and a friend we have in common said that she was interested in working with me again and that I should go for it. I was a little nervous approaching her for my first film but thankfully she said yes. I learned a tremendous amount from her. She is incredibly professional and I rate her as one of the most gifted actors of her generation. It was a daunting process to be honest and I knew that she would have a strong opinion on what we were doing but she was actually very helpful to me, both during the rehearsals and during the actual filming. The final scene in the film where she walks out of the house we did just once and on the second day of shooting. Unbelievable.

JW: *This is one of Sam Riley's very first acting roles. How did he convince you? He doesn't do an impression of Curtis. He tries to capture his spirit.*

AC: When I met Sam he struck me as a dead ringer for Ian Curtis so that was an immediate attraction. Talking to him I felt a freshness and a non-actor quality that I was really searching for. Sam has an incredible personality and I knew that he would bring a lot of himself. Sam also comes from the North of England so shared a certain similarity with Ian. When preparing the film I often watched Ken Loach's *Kes* and I was struck by David Bradley. I couldn't believe that I was watching an actor. I was hoping that Sam would bring some of this to the screen. Sam also stood his ground against Samantha and I think they are great together.

JW: *The surviving members of Joy Division were very keen that you get the portrayal of Rob Gretton right. He was obviously a major factor in their lives.*

AC: Toby Kebbell was terrific in the audition. He put on these huge glasses and was naturally very funny. I had seen him in *Dead Man's Shoes*. Toby is totally natural and his delivery is terrific. He thought of a couple of lines on the spot. Quite a few people that are portrayed in the film have passed away and it is very important to get these people right. Steve Morris was especially concerned that Rob Gretton came across as likeable. His language is coarse but you can tell that he had a really good heart.

JW: *There is a humour to the film too. Gretton's line 'Cheer up. You could be in The Fall' is priceless.*

AC: The humour was important to me. The camaraderie too. The actors that played Bernard Sumner, Peter Hook and Stephen Morris all had to learn their instruments to the degree that it would look believable during playback. They were so determined to get it right and practised everyday. In the end they could play just as well as Joy Division. That is according to New Order's manager by the way. The side effect of the actors rehearsing as band was that the dynamic of a real band found its way on screen. It also made the live band scenes more authentic.

JW: *In many ways the film is about escape and the search for freedom.*

AC: That is something that is very personal to me. I was born in a small village on a small island and so escape has been a big part of my life. As I said, I didn't want to just make a film about Joy Division so all the other elements – the love, the struggle, health problems – were incredibly important to me. I also wanted to show how out of mundane circumstances something very beautiful can grow.

JW: *Because Manchester has changed so radically you were unable to use many of the original locations. Where did you end up filming?*

AC: Mainly in Nottingham. Architecturally it is similar. We also spent three days in Macclesfield and the house where you see Ian and Debbie living is the real house in which they lived. The walk that Ian does to his place of work is a real walk filmed in real time.

JW: *You had to finance the film yourself initially. I imagine financiers were wary of a film that marked the first feature of its director, its lead actor and its cinematographer, Martin Ruhe.*

AC: It was painful. A lot of the things that put people off are actually what makes the film so great. At least people seem to think so. All I could think about was that I wanted to make a film that people would want to see. I thought it would be my one shot at directing so I decided to go for it. At one point we had everything together, the cast, the locations and then we had no money. I decided to mortgage everything and I am pleased that I did. It turned out to be an incredible experience. The first screening in Cannes was beyond belief. To see people reacting so positively…

JW: *The film looks striking too. Did you always intend to shoot in black and white? And did your outsider status contribute to the aesthetic?*

AC: The collective memory of Joy Division is black and white. Very few photographs exist of them in colour. Also, their actual output was black and white. I am thinking here of their album covers. When I came to England originally, I found it quite bleak so for these reasons black and white made sense. Martin Ruhe is German and I am Dutch and although the setting and the story is very English the perspective is perhaps more European.

Florian **Henckel von Donnersmarck**

A remarkably assured first feature from the maker of the award-winning shorts *Dobermann* (1999) and *The Crusader* (2002), writer-director Florian Henckel von Donnersmarck's *The Lives of Others* (2006) paints a dark picture of life under the Communist regime in East Germany. Eschewing a purely historical approach by creating fictional characters, the film is part-thriller and part-love story, and offers a compelling tale of individuals whose lives and search for dignity are shaped by the society in which they live. The film also shows with remarkable consistency that the mechanisms which upheld the GDR ultimately led to its demise.

Von Donnersmarck spent four years conducting intensive research and writing his screenplay before beginning shooting. In addition to reading an abundance of specialised literature, the director also spent countless hours in conversation with eyewitnesses, and former Stasi (State Police) employees and their victims. He was advised and supported on historical matters by a number of distinguished specialists, including Prof. Manfred Wilke, head of the Research Committee on the SED (Sozialistische Einheitspartei Deutschlands, the Socialist Unity Party), Jörg Drieselmann, head of the Research Agency and Memorial in Normannenstrasse and former Stasi colonel Wolfgang Schmidt.

Further establishing time, place and texture was von Donnersmarck's determination to shoot wherever possible on original locations. These venues include the former Stasi headquarters in Normannenstrasse, a feared address during the years of the SED regime. *The Lives of Others* was also the first and is, to date, the only feature film that was allowed to be shot in the original file-card archives of the former Stasi headquarters.

Awarded the grade 'particularly worthwhile' by the German Film Evaluation Bureau, *The Lives of Others*' list of accolades also includes the Best Foreign Language Film Academy Award, seven Lola German Film Awards and three

European Film Awards.

This interview was previously published in *Projections 5+ The European Film Academy* (Faber, 2007). The director has since completed the disappointing *The Tourist* (2010).

―――――

JASON WOOD: *Let's start with the quote from Lenin.*

FLORIAN HENCKEL VON DONNERSMARCK: The quote from Lenin was really the starting point. I remember very clearly the moment when I had the idea to make the film. Listening to a Beethoven piano sonata and I remember this quote I read in a book by Maxim Gorky, actually a friend of Lenin's, and Lenin had said to him 'Beethoven's appassionato is my favourite piece of music, but I don't want to listen to it anymore because it makes me go all soft, stroke peoples' heads and tell them sweet, stupid things. But I have to smash in those heads. Smash them in without mercy in order to finish my revolution.' And I thought perhaps I should find a film story or plot where I can force Lenin to listen to the appassionato just as he was getting ready to smash in somebody's head. And would that change the course of history? When I thought about forcing Lenin to listen to the music I had the story within a few minutes, the entire structure, and I sat down at my keyboard and typed it within an hour. So that was a two-page outline of the plot and that still is remarkably close to what I ended up writing. It's just that it took another three years.

JW: *Let's talk about those three years. You had made a number of shorts before this that were very highly regarded which makes this an audacious undertaking for a first feature, particularly the scope and the attention to detail. Tell me about the three-year research period, what kind of processes you went through and why the need for such accuracy?*

FD: I knew all of the survivors of that period were still alive so I knew if I got anything wrong I would be slaughtered. As a filmmaker it is a matter of honour to get the setting for a film right. Even if most of the survivors of the Russian revolution were dead by then I'm sure the makers of *Dr. Zhivago* [1965] adopted exactly the same painstaking work to get the details right. There's something comically wrong with a film if you don't work on those details. Before writing the first line of dialogue I spent one and a half years just researching. I didn't intend for it to take that long but it was only after one and a half years that I reached a point where I really knew enough about it to tell the tale objectively. And I'd heard both sides and so many contradictions in the ways that the stories were told about this that the point had come where I had enough to make my own mind up about how it was.

I'd talked to Stasi victims and to Stasi officers. It was quite an emotional rollercoaster ride that year and a half. Literally, I'd be meeting one of the victims in the morning that would tell me about how they were tortured psychologically and in the afternoon I'd meet the person who did all that. I actually invited my main Stasi consultant to the film. Luckily he didn't come in uniform. He came with his wife who was also a Stasi officer. They were only allowed to marry amongst themselves. I was watching him out of the corner of my eye. He left immediately after the film was over and I thought that would be the last I ever heard from him but then he wrote me a letter. 'I'm glad at least you got the historical details right. But isn't it a sad state of things that the only way you can portray a Stasi officer as a hero is by making him a traitor?' I thought it was incredible that he can have seen the film that you have seen and still be thinking 'what a traitor!' It was absurd.

JW: *There was some interest in the film early on from financiers but am I correct in saying they wanted you to write it as a comedy?*

FD: Well, there had been a number of successful comedies treating this period in German history. *Good Bye Lenin!* [2003] for example. They read the screenplay and didn't know what to do with it and thought that as there were comic elements in my short films....

JW: *I was going to save this unil the end but it seems apt now to mention it, but is there a certain amount of vindication on your part.*

FD: Vindication has such a negative connotation. I try not to focus on the people who made it hard for me but on those who fought with me. Everyone you saw in that long end credit. Those were people who were prepared to work for much less than they make and the actors even more so. I was relieved when the film did well that I kept calling the distributor in Germany, who again kept telling me that no one was going to want to watch this. By this point I still needed about 130,000 Euros on lab work to finish the film. So I knew I wouldn't even be able to finish it if I didn't get a distributor to put up that money. They all refused. Even the arthouse distributors. In the end it was the largest German distributor who picked up the film, knowing that everyone else had refused this film. They didn't know what to do so they just tested the film with an audience of a certain level of education and it did very well. And as a result of that they did it.

JW: *Ulrich Muhe has an explicit connection with the material.*

FD: Muhe was probably the most formidable actor of the former GDR, and at a very young age became incredibly famous and was at the Deuschte-teatr in East Berlin. He received all the main roles and Heiner Muller even constructed entire theatre evenings around him and considered him the greatest actor ever. But for this film he didn't prepare at all. His only preparation he told me was to remember. After *The Lives of Others* he claimed his Stasi files. Every victim has the right to do so, although fewer than ten per cent have chosen to do so. He found out that four members of his theatre group, which for an actor is like his family, were actually placed there by the Stasi to monitor him, to write reports on him. And he also found out, and perhaps the most painful discovery, was his wife of six years had been listed as an informer and had been reporting on him.

He's a very sensitive man and in the interview I did with him to accompany the published screenplay I told him that these are things the tabloid press will find out and will be grossly misrepresented, so why don't you tell me the story from your perspective? And he did. And we took twenty pages to properly cover the subject. And most people thought we had gone too far, washing dirty laundry in public. And he was attacked very severely. In some parts he was hailed as finally the person to cross that bridge and talk about these things. But it was really a very painful thing for him. He really couldn't enjoy the success of this film because of the vicious attacks. Every day the answering machine would be full of the most awful venom. And all he was saying was 'I want to be able to talk about my past when people ask me. I have nothing to be ashamed of.' He said something interesting in that in dictatorships he says they force their victims to be silent out of a sense of shame. Often Jews who experienced something similar in the concentration camps speak of not talking about it out of a sense of shame, some weird malfunction in the brain that makes you ashamed of injustices that you have suffered. Many victims of child abuse know about that. And he said he didn't want that to happen to him, he wanted to talk about these things. He suffered, so much so that he really is not in good health now.

JW: *A key moment in the film is when Wiesler goes to Dreyman's apartment and discovers Brecht for the first time.*

FD: He sees everything with different eyes. It's the first time he's not there to intimidate or to install wires and he sees that these people have lives. It's the scene that I'm most proud of. It takes only perhaps a minute and a half and it has no dialogue but you can see how this person is searching for meaning and searching for feeling, but he has been repressed for so long that he doesn't know how to go about it. He thought that he could find feeling by ordering a prostitute but this is unable to satisfy him and then he realises that these people are finding satisfaction through art so maybe this is something he should be doing; he thinks that maybe he should be reading Brecht.

JW: *Do you think that this is the specific moment that he decides his life should take a different direction?*

FD: I don't think that there is a specific moment. I just think that he is gradually being pushed away from the path that he felt that was the right path and that perhaps he was mistaken. He doesn't really know what he is to do but that what he is doing so far isn't right. It's like a mid-life crisis but only in a good way. It was always important to me that there not be one specific turning point.

On the one hand, on the Stasi side he realises that his sacred mission to find enemies of the state is being used for personal motives and this central committee member just has a passion for this girl. He also realises that his friend, who was always a little less intelligent and a little less party loyal than he, is making a better career and that people actually mistrust him for being almost religious in his support of the party.

On the other hand, as he is monitoring the so-called enemies of the state, he has to ask himself 'are these really the people I've been fighting against all my life?' They seem so normal to him, especially as he experiences them in moments of greatness and moments of weakness. These moments always seemed easier to ignore in an interrogation scenario. There is also a third level that leads to change and that is art. He experiences that it is possible to live with music and to live with poetry and he realises that it is possible for him to live with these things too. All these things together gradually make him change. As the change is gradual – he is a resistant hero at first, letting things go and falsifying reports – it is only right at the end that he decides to do something physically to help Dreyman. People often don't feel they are that heroic when they are doing heroic acts, it is often only in retrospect that they recognise their heroism.

JW: *Adding to the texture, and in line with your requiring that though a work of fiction the film is grounded in historical accuracy, was your decision to shoot on location wherever possible. Given the amount of changes in so short a period this must have been quite an undertaking.*

FD: It was harder to shoot something in 1984 East Berlin than it would have been to make a film set in Renaissance Italy for example. At least if you go into other periods of history you have buildings that have been preserved exactly that way. In Germany, since 1989, people have done nothing but tried to destroy traces of that period. Fortunately, we got some very special authorisations to shoot in the

Stasi archives so what you see in the film are the real Stasi files and archives and the real rooms with their revolving index-card machines. I also found an apartment that had not been renovated, enabling me to get the texture of the walls. This always looks more authentic to me than if you try to build something in a studio.

What was really hard to find was the street outside Dreyman's apartment because I needed that as a 360 degrees location. The graffiti was everywhere and there was of course no graffiti in the GDR. Every morning we had to have a group of painters re-paint the walls of this entire street because every night the graffiti would just re-appear. Our producers even calculated to see if it would be cheaper to employ armed security guards for our clean walls overnight or to just have painters re-paint from 4am to 7am every morning. We decided to do the latter.

I really tried to reconstruct that world and by looking at pictures I realised that red and blue, two colours that seem the most shocking to the eye and which have very extreme qualities to them, were largely absent. It occurred to me that we could reconstruct the East by simply leaving out these two colours all together. That's what I did. I experimented through drawings and designs and when I showed these and shots from the film to my friends and relatives from the East they remarked right away that it really reminded them of the GDR. I stuck to that principle and there is no red or blue in the film. I think that the film is very evocative of the GDR because of this. Of course, there was red and blue in the GDR but eliminating them made it feel more like the GDR than it would if you reconstructed things exactly as they were. When the lead actors and I toured the film for several weeks in the East people just could not believe how they were able to re-enter their past. I decided not to tell them about my little trick with colour.

Fernando **Eimbcke**

A graduate of Mexico's highly regarded Centro Universitario de Estudios Cinematográficos, Fernando Eimbcke announced his arrival with the enormously likeable and charming Duck Season (*Temporada de Patos*, 2004).

Flama and Moko are fourteen years old and have everything ready for a perfect Sunday afternoon: a parentless apartment, videogames and money for a pizza delivery. However, a sequence of seemingly unconnected events and interruptions soon conspire against them. Set almost entirely within an apartment block on the outskirts of Mexico City and using largely inexperienced teenage actors, the film offers a salutary lesson in adolescent friendship and love. A triumph of economy, the film is reminiscent of the early work of Jim Jarmusch.

Eimbcke's follow up won the FIPRESCI prize at the Berlin Film Festival. Sharing some of the themes of his debut, *Lake Tahoe* (2008) is a little more enigmatic in its consideration of the uneasy passage from adolescence to adulthood.

Set in a small harbour town, the film unfolds during a single day and begins with a resolutely non-dramatic car crash. The car in question belongs to sixteen-year-old Juan, who escapes his family problems by cruising around in his parent's shiny new vehicle. During his attempts to find a mechanic, Juan has a number of escapades involving a lethargic dog-loving repairman, a punkish young waif with an infant son, and a Bruce Lee-obsessed teenager who turns out to be an expert in all things mechanical.

This beautifully judged and deftly directed coming-of-age tale confirms Eimbcke as one of the brightest voices in Mexican's cinema's current crop of emerging young talents.

JASON WOOD: Lake Tahoe *was developed with the support of the Sundance Screenwriter's Lab. How did this process assist you and how many changes did the script go through before you had a version that you knew you wanted to bring to the screen?*

FERNANDO EIMBCKE: In the lab Paula Markovitch [co-writer] and I worked with different advisors; every one of them gave us very good ideas, but definitely the work with John Lee Hancock [*Perfect World*] was amazing. He showed us our own script in a new perspective. The script had a lot of drafts, but when I say a lot it means a lot! And at the end the final draft was very similar to the first draft. I think I needed to make that kind of search.

JW: *Your second feature following* Temporada de Patos, *what experience were you able to bring to this project having already had one feature under your belt and what similarities and differences, if any, do you see between the two films?*

FE: When I finished *Temporada de Patos* I thought I had learned something about screenwriting, actor's direction and how and where to put the camera. But when I wrote and shot *Lake Tahoe* I found myself like a first-time film writer/director and I would like to continue working in every future film like in the first one. I don't want to be a 'pro'. Sounds strange but I want to make every film with the fears and doubts I had in the first film; in some way those fears and doubts propels my creativity.

About the similarities between *Temporada* and *Tahoe*, both of them are melodrama with a slight farcical tone, but in *Temporada* the farcical tone was heavier. About the differences, the protagonist in *Lake Tahoe* deals with a stronger conflict than the *Temporada* characters. *Lake Tahoe* is a kind of road movie, while *Temporada* is like an anti-road movie. *Lake Tahoe* is about one character while *Temporada* deals with a choral structure.

JW: *I think I'm right in stating that you are a graduate of the prestigious Centro Universitario de Estudios Cinematográficos, one of many excellent film schools Mexico boasts. How essential is the school for young filmmakers in Mexico, and what role has it played in producing another remarkable generation of Mexican filmmakers?*

FE: Yes I studied at the CUEC, and as far as I know there aren't so many film schools in Mexico, there's the CUEC, the Centro de Capacitación Cinematográfica and some universities like the Iberoamericana have a kind of film programmw, but not as a career. I think that film schools are good for some people; for me it was very useful, and a lot of great filmmakers like Alfonso Cuarón and Julián

Hernández studied in the film schools, but I don't think is essential. A lot of the best filmmakers in México like Carlos Reygadas and Alejandro González Iñárritu never went to a film school.

JW: Lake Tahoe *won the FIPRESCI prize at the Berlin Film Festival. How much did this award mean to you on a personal level and in terms of enhancing your reputation outside of Mexico, how significant do you consider the award to be?*

FE: On a personal level a prize means recognition of the work of all the crew that worked on the film. And as director I feel very proud and thankful. A prize helps the film to get attention, and that's invaluable with an independent film with unknown actors. A prize can help you to find funds for your next film, but at the end I find kind of strange the prize system. I mean, to decide which film is better than another? We're not talking about football where two teams play to demonstrate who's better; we're talking about films. I don't think a film is better than another, they're just different. But when you apply to a festival you accept this prize system. But also, when the film wins a prize I turn into the happiest person.

JW: *The setting of the film is very important and you make much of the somewhat sleepy, smalltown environment. Where exactly did you set the film and what aspects of your location did you particularly wish to emphasise?*

FE: The film was shot in Progreso, Yucatán, in the southeast part of Mexico. Alexis Zabé, the cinematographer, proposed the location. When I wrote the script I thought of an arid place, an industrial place, but when Alexis read the script he proposed a tropical place. I asked him why, if this story talked about the dead, and he told me that he found a story about death but also a story about life. In Progreso we found that kind of aridness/dead and tropical/life kind of feeling.

JW: *Amongst the many subjects central to* Lake Tahoe *is the difficult transition from adolescence to adulthood. Diego Cataño, with whom you have worked previously and who strikes me as one of the most interesting actors at work today, conveys this notion beautifully. Could you just say something about Diego and what directions you gave him in terms of creating his character?*

FE: Diego is a great actor. He's really young but very intelligent, sensitive and generous. His idea of acting is to make the character in front of him exist. If the character in front of him exists, he exists. His idea of acting is about generosity.

About the direction I gave him. If you trust in the conflict you gave the character in the script then you don't need to say too many things to the actor. Diego understood in a very clear way what Juan's character wanted: to desperately escape.

JW: *The film is obviously filled with a very interesting cross-section of people and types and seemingly random incidents. These include a lethargic dog-loving repairman, Lucia, the punkish young waif with an infant son, and a Bruce Lee-obsessed technical whiz kid. How do you feel, if at all, each helps Juan come to understand his grief and to understand that sometimes in life inexplicable events occur?*

FE: Even though *Tahoe* doesn't work in a choral structure Paula and I were really concerned to build the other characters with a conflict. Those conflicts resonate in a special way in Juan's character because after his loss his perception of the world is completely different. The most important thing for Paula and me was that the characters and their conflicts help Juan without knowing it. The characters and their conflicts are in some way absurd and inexplicable, like death.

JW: *The film is very precise in terms of composition. Can you say more about your favouring of quite static shots and your collaborative work with Alexis Zabé, another in a long line of excellent technicians from Mexico?*

FE: I don't know why. I just don't like to move the camera. Maybe I don't have an elaborate kind of cinematography mind, so I imagined the scenes in the simplest way and I tried to be faithful to that until the end. Alexis, is one of the best cinematographers in the world. I learned from him. He's not just a DP; he's an artist, a true artist. He helped me with the script, the cast, everything. He's very intelligent, sensitive and stubborn, a fact that I'm extremely thankful for. I don't like to work with people who say yes to everything I say.

JW: *Critics are quick to compare you with Jim Jarmusch. Is the reference flattering or tiresome? Are there other directors from who you draw inspiration? Ozu seems to have a bearing on your unhurried visual aesthetic.*

FE: About the Jarmusch comparison, I grew up in a non-cinematic family, I didn't go to the movies so often, but I remember that on Sunday mornings I used to see on television Laurel and Hardy, that sense of humour, that simplicity and the melancholic black and white made a deep impression on me. All my friends were into *Star Wars*; I never saw *Star Wars* until I was thirty years old, and I accept it is a good film, but it didn't make an impact on me. When I was at film school a friend of mine showed me *Stranger Than Paradise* [1984] and I found in the film a sense of humour, a simplicity, and a melancholic black and white that transported me to those Sunday mornings. Then I had the chance to see Ozu's *Tokyo Story* [1953] on 35mm; the feeling I experienced in that screening is the reason why I make films. The other film that inspired *Lake Tahoe* was De Sica's *Bicycle Thieves* [1948]. I wanted to make a film where the objective was really simple like a bike or a car but the meaning behind that object was really deep.

JW: *Like your compatriot Carlos Reygadas, you seem to be very fond of enigmatic titles. Was* Lake Tahoe *always going to be the sticker on the car bumper at the end or did you toy with other destinations?*

FE: Lake Tahoe was always a sticker on the car bumper. The name appeared in the first treatment as 'Do you remember Lake Tahoe?' I love Raymond Carver and the title sounded to me like a Carver title; it was like a kind of tribute. At the end I decided to named it just *Lake Tahoe*, because when we were shooting the film people asked us what was the name of the film, and when we answered 'Do you remember Lake Tahoe?' they responded very confused, 'No I don't remember Lake Tahoe.'

Michel **Gondry**

Noted for his incredibly inventive visual style and off-kilter view of the harsher realities of romance, the feature films of Michel Gondry are augmented by a series of equally idiosyncratic and eye-popping commercials, gallery installations and music videos. His work with Björk is particularly memorable.

Gondry's first feature was the disappointing *Human Nature* (2001) but he bounced back with *Eternal Sunshine of the Spotless Mind* (2004), a second collaboration with screenwriter Charlie Kaufman. The film echoed Gondry's work in other media with its arresting mix of state-of-the-art visual effects and more DIY aesthetic. For all the infectious energy of the film, the story of a couple undergoing a procedure to erase themselves from each other's memories is underpinned with a melancholy and sense of loss that recurs again and again throughout Gondry's work. It is certainly at the forefront of *The Science of Sleep* (2006), the film around which the following interview took place.

An astonishing roller-coaster ride through a humane, all too human consciousness, the film was the director's first from his own screenplay. Shy, inhibited Stéphane's (Gael García Bernal) life finally takes off when his mother convinces him to go back to France – the land of his childhood – where a marvellous job apparently awaits him. Possessed of a lively imagination, Stéphane's eccentric dream world always threatens to engulf his real life. Bitterly disappointed when the job does not live up to his expectations, a new acquaintance in the shape of his attractive neighbour, Stéphanie (Charlotte Gainsbourg), helps him to get over his doldrums. Before long he falls in love with this young woman whose fantasy unquestionably matches his own. Things that were once the stuff of only his wildest dreams now appear to be turning into reality, and he looks forward to a happy, magical future. And yet, at the very moment when the publication of a calendar containing his drawings bodes well for his career, he suddenly has the impression that Stéphanie is rejecting him. Or is he misinterpreting something? Is it merely his insecurity rearing its ugly head again? Torn between his dreams and reality, Stéphane begins to realise that both worlds are spiralling out of control… Anchored by an outstanding performance from García Bernal that's funny and moving, he provides the perfect canvas for Gondry's ceaseless energy and imagination.

Since completing *The Science of Sleep* Gondry has remained incredibly productive. There was the terrifically entertaining documentary *Dave Chappelle's Block Party* (2006), *Be Kind Rewind* (2008) in which two bumbling video-store clerks (played by Jack Black and Mos Def) inadvertently erase the footage from all of the tapes in their video rental store. In order to keep the business running, they re-shoot every film in the store with their own camera, with a budget of zero dollars, and another documentary, the incredibly personal *The Thorn in the Heart* (2009). The disappointment of *The Green Hornet* (2011), a multi-budget superhero misfire, was quickly erased by the more modest and affecting documentary *The We and the I* (2012), a look at the lives of a group of teenagers who ride the same bus route and how their relationships change and evolve on the last day of school.

JASON WOOD: The Science of Sleep *is your first film from your own screenplay. What difference did this make in terms of freeing up your creativity?*

MICHEL GONDRY: I needed this freedom because I was describing dreams and I wanted to be able to not have to explain them. If you work with a screenwriter or a studio you need to explain everything and intellectualise everything and I wanted the freedom to not have to do this. There is a danger that when you explain everything you can lose some deeper meaning. When your brain takes over you lose something from your emotions. The only way to do this film was to write it and direct it myself and get as much freedom as possible. Ultimately I was able to achieve this. I also had to find actors that could play their parts with complete trust in me. The downside of all this of course is that I often had to confront myself and deal with my own insecurities.

JW: *How much did you draw on instances from your own life? You filmed in the apartment block where you grew up. Was delving back into your past difficult?*

MG: I kind of enjoyed it. I wanted to be respectful and I also didn't want to lay all the blame on Stéphanie. I didn't want her to be too mean and I don't think she is. In real life she was not always so nice. It was interesting to remember details and conversations and bring them back to life with these actors.

JW: *The film explores the intersection between dream and reality and also, perhaps most pertinently, the drudgery of working in mundane jobs and not being able to realise your creativity.*

MG: This is something I experienced. When you end up with a creative job and you are dissatisfied it is good to think back to the mundane jobs that you have done as it makes you realise how lucky you are. If I had started off with a creative role or gone into directing straight away I could be slightly spoiled. When I do become frustrated all I have to do is think back. It's important to go through these dirty jobs and be miserable for a while.

JW: *I loved Stéphane's TV show. It's a kind of tollbooth between his waking life and his flights of fancy from reality.*

MG: The initial script didn't have this element. I only incorporated it after a few years. It's a natural process. You start in reality and then you are on your bed and you close your eyes and you start to sink and talk to yourself and suddenly you are in your dreams. I thought of Stéphane TV as being like a kind of antechamber, or a purgatory. I didn't want to use voiceover; it has been done too many times in movies so I came up with the idea of this TV show. It also enabled me to show another side of Stephane. Much more composed, confident and charismatic. This contrasts with his shyness in his dai;y life.

JW: *The film also replicates those instances that occur in life where you cannot recall if you have dreamed something or if it actually happened. Did you want there to be room for consideration of what is real and what has occurred in the subconscious?*

MG: I did not want there to be confusion. I wanted people to know when they are in a dream and when they are in reality. What was important for me was capturing the notion of Stephane and Stephanie sharing the same vision, or, as we say, sharing the same dream. To me it's a sign of love and its very romantic. This is true even at the end of the film. Despite all the anger they have towards each other they still have this romantic connection.

JW: *And yet there is a disconnect. When Stéphane shows Stéphanie the 3D glasses she comments that real life is in 3D anyway.*

MG: For him imagination, creativity and love are the same feeling. It is all one feeling and he cannot separate them. He loves her because she allows him to be himself and to be creative but by being himself he becomes too intense for her and shows a lack of confidence to her that is unattractive. She actually tells him that it is not attractive for a guy to cry. This is something that I have also been told. By a girl I had a crush on.

JW: *Gael Garcia Bernal is very fearless as an actor. His part here is often unflattering.*

MG: He brought a great sense of humour to it all. We talked a lot before we shot and for about a year we discussed how the movie would be conceived. We came to know each other very well and this is perhaps one of the most satisfying elements of the filmmaking process, getting to know your collaborators. We both felt safe to try anything. On the first take I would often not give him any direction just to see how he would surprise me and he did, more often than not.

JW: *You often have everyday objects turning up in unexpected places. This reminds me of one of the motifs of the surrealists. Is this a movement that influenced you?*

MG: Yes, in the sense that I like them and they are one of the most interesting movements in France and perhaps also the most creative. They also talk about dreams in a similar way to how I talk about my dreams. Talking about dreams makes me feel close to them but I wouldn't necessarily equate myself too closely with the surrealists. The thing I do admire about the surrealists, and it's a broad family that also includes figures such as Tex Avery and Charlie Chaplin, is that they are unconventional and very much exist in their own right.

JW: *And do you delve into your own unconscious a great deal for your work?*

MG: I do but I am a little wary of the word 'unconscious'. Psychoanalysts like to use it quite often, to my mind, to get power over their patients. I prefer to think of it as the symbolism of dreams.

JW: *I like the aesthetic of the film. It's a push and pull between cutting-edge technology and a sort of naivety.*

MG: I like to challenge myself to approach technically difficult tasks but I also like the idea of people being able to see how something is made. The CGI makes everything invisible and because it is coming from a computer I always feel that you never really believe that any reality has been created. I have nothing against computer-generated imagery but it's a bit like punk music. I like to see the chords and how they are being played. There can be a more direct connection when you see how something is done. I also like the idea of seeing something and wanting to go home and try it yourself. I see this in my son. When he goes to see certain movies or certain bands he gets inspired and it is often the less technically complex films or musicians that inspire him.

JW: *And you shot the majority of the dream sequences first.*

MG: Correct. You can't do these whilst you are busy shooting. It would be impossible. Also, for me you can tell when the actors are acting in front of a blue screen. They just seem a little dead. It's far better to project the animation behind the actors. They can see what is going on and be part of the process. To achieve that I have to shoot the dream sequences first.

JW: *Does the fact that you work in other disciplines help your filmmaking?*

MG: I like to work hard and in other disciplines because I lack self-confidence. I need self-discipline and this enables me to make up for my naivety. My father was always calling me naïve. My producer has started doing it too.

Joanna **Hogg**

Joanna Hogg started her career as a photographer before becoming interested in the moving image. She attended film school in the UK and, after several short films, became a prolific director of television drama. Hogg used this as a testing ground for developing her aesthetic as a filmmaker, and in particular working with actors to obtain performances of authenticity and depth.

Unrelated (2007), Hogg's feature debut, won critical acclaim and numerous awards, including the FIPRESCI International Critics' Award at the London Film Festival in 2007, the *Guardian* First Film Award and the *Evening Standard* Most Promising Newcomer award in 2009. An examination of bourgeois values amongst an upper-class family holidaying in Tuscany, the film was remarkable for its naturalistic performances and frills-free aesthetic. A film of silences and recriminations, it slowly worked its way under the skin and announced the arrival of a major new British filmmaking talent.

Archipelago (2010) was the equally assured follow up. The film follows the travails of an upper-class family holidaying in Tresco and again looks at what happens to the carefully calibrated equilibrium when simmering resentments rise to the fore. In many ways a deft comedy of manners, the film is refreshing in its honest portrait of upper-class values and concerns. It also established Hogg's close working association with fast-rising young British actor Tom Hiddleston.

Exhibition is Hogg's third feature. A portrait of a relationship in stasis, it stars Viv Albertine and Liam Gillick, and is the final part of what the director considers to be a trilogy.

JASON WOOD: *You've described* Archipelago *as being less autobiographical than* Unrelated *but more personal.*

JOANNA HOGG: I would say *Archipelago* is not autobiographical in that it is not based on an account of my own life. *Unrelated* was more directly inspired by a specific moment in time which I had experienced.

Archipelago sprung more from my imagination. However, I was concerned that by using my imagination in this way, the characters and story would be somehow untrue to my own thoughts and feelings. Actually this was not the case and in some ways it helped me to get even closer to the 'truth'. I am learning to use my imagination more but it continues to be a challenge. The ideas are still based on my own emotional experience. But this avoidance of expressing a literal truth is very freeing, and opens up so many more worlds and possibilities.

A different facet of myself inspired each character in *Archipelago*. Cynthia is based on a part of myself that is controlling and intolerant. Edward is based on a more indecisive, over-sensitive aspect of myself and so on… I am fascinated by how such contradictory traits can exist in one person.

JW: *What did Tresco contribute to* Archipelago *both in terms of atmosphere and its physical characteristics?*

JH: Landscape gives form to my imagination. It is a springboard into the story. Actually the landscape is the story. I want it to mirror the characters' feelings and emotions. I cannot separate the landscape of Tresco from the story. One wouldn't have happened without the other.

I already knew Tresco from my childhood. It was a place I grew up in, through years of going there for Easter holidays. Its associations were happy ones and I surprised myself that *Archipelago* shows a darker, more melancholy side of the island.

This island fascinates me because it has a dreamlike quality due to a kind of condensation of the landscape. There are quasi-surreal juxtapositions which I haven't seen anywhere else. On the one hand, in the north you have wild moorland such as you would find in the highlands of Scotland and on the other, a lush tropical landscape that's more characteristic of Cornwall.

JW: *In* Archipelago *as in* Unrelated *you use no incidental music.*

JH: I absolutely love music but in cinema it is an incredibly powerful tool which needs to be handled very carefully. You can show an image of a flowerpot, but coupled with a Wagner opera, it can spring to life and be very emotional. So it's an easy trick to use and most films, for my taste, use it far too often.

Exhibition, Joanna Hogg, 2013 (Wild Horses/BFI/BBC)

I also love natural sounds. I am very aware of them in everyday life and enjoy recording them. I have a particular fondness for birdsong, though like certain music, I can find it excruciatingly sad. For *Archipelago* I wanted to explore the idea of birdsong and communication. I liked the idea of counter-pointing the awkward silences between the Leighton family with the constant chattering of birds.

JW: *You strike a successful balance between actors and non-professionals such as Amy Lloyd and Christopher Baker.*

JH: The idea to cast Tom Hiddleston again and also to write a part for Christopher Baker, my painting teacher, arrived around the same time. Yet I had no idea how the two characters would converge or even if they would be in the same story. I enjoy observing people and imagining how I might place them in a film. It's a kind of 'game' I play with non-professional actors and can result in the beginnings of a story.

I like the way the actor and the non-actor communicate with each other. I want the actor to stop acting and I find the non-actor helps this to happen. Actors' tricks don't work so well with a non-professional. The actor is forced to use their instincts and be in the moment. Of course, if you're not careful, it can work the other way round and you find the non-actor wants to start acting!

For the character of Rose, I knew I wanted to find a professional cook. I interviewed many cooks before finally meeting Amy Lloyd. It turned out that

Archipelago was Amy's first film role and her first professional job as a cook. This part was a real leap of faith for her. She knew nothing about the story when she agreed to play Rose, and was brave enough to remain in the dark, pretty much throughout the shoot.

JW: *Edward strikes me as a man completely shackled to his family, and the notion of family, yet desperate to attain a sense of personal freedom. Was this a concept that interested you?*

JH: Edward and how he is in relation to his family is at the centre of what is interesting to me about this story. This theme is the heartbeat of the film and one I suspect I will continue to explore in future films.

I had an inspiring conversation with Tom, when I was first thinking about the character of Edward. We were talking about how a sense of oneself can so easily vanish in the family fold; the struggle to keep hold of oneself when your family refuses to acknowledge you are an individual and an adult.

JW: *For all the tension and awkwardness in* Archipelago *there is also a sense of humour at play.*

JH: I was aware during the making of *Archipelago*, and then during the editing, that the tension in some of the scenes was very funny. I think the humour comes out of those situations that are so uncomfortable and awkward, that laughter is the only response. It wasn't a conscious decision to make *Archipelago* funnier, but it has a darker tone than *Unrelated*, and I relish depicting awkward and embarrassing social situations. These situations naturally become so uncomfortable, you just have to laugh. I love that audiences have been laughing during screenings of *Archipelago*. I find it is a very satisfying response.

JW: *I understand that the two films form part of a trilogy. What plans have you got for the conclusion?*

JH: I am returning to themes of childlessness begun in *Unrelated*, combined with continued exploration into what family means. I am getting flashes of something that is highly coloured, crowded with people and more physical with a redemptive, optimistic outlook…

JW: *What were some of the thought processes behind* Exhibition *and what were the main topics and themes that you set out to explore?*

JH: I'll play around with ideas for months before I settle on my story. Then something takes hold and ideas begin to pull together. With each film I am engaging my imagination more. This time I tapped into my dreams and pushed myself further in terms of a less linear narrative and creating different levels of reality.

Actually it was this process of creation that I wanted to depict in the film. It's quite rare in films to see people working and I wanted to see an artist during the act of creation. To show inspiration in motion and how sexually charged this can be. But to offset this with the challenges of being in a relationship and the different roles required to keep everything in balance, especially from a woman's point of view.

Above all I wanted to depict this marriage from the inside out, and it felt like riskier territory for me as it was naturally going to connect with my own personal life. So I needed to find a way of visualising the story which would create some distance between myself and my characters. The house, which I had encountered through my friendship with the architect James Melvin, seemed to be the perfect container for my story.

JW: *When we have spoken previously you had always described* Unrelated *and* Archipelago *as forming part of a trilogy. How does* Exhibition *complete that trilogy and how do you see the films fitting together as a whole?*

JH: I hate saying goodbye to my films. Hanging onto elements from the previous film is one way to make this transition easier. After *Archipelago* I thought I would go back and see what the relationship between Anna and Alex from *Unrelated* might be like back home in London. I had finished *Archipelago* wishing I had explored Edward's sexuality, so then this gets pushed into the next film. A lot of time passes between the films and my ideas are changing and adapting and responding to new situations. I never look back at my work so I don't know how they look in relationship to one another.

JW: *Again, in the context of all three films, you described* Unrelated *as being party biographical,* Archipelago *as less biographical but more personal. Where does* Exhibition *stand in all this?*

JH: Did I?! Actually I'd say now that none of them are biographical but all of them are personal – in very different ways. In the end I'm unable to say what is personal and what is not. It's not relevant to the films and anyway I forget. Even if it starts off as intensely personal it ends up just being the film. I have to divorce myself from it, in order to keep my sanity and move on the next…

JW: *An obvious question I know but can you take me through the casting* process? You have always adopted a very original approach so I just wanted to learn more about how you arrived at Liam Gillick and Viv Albertine, both of whom are terrific in their roles. Also, what chemistry, or lack of, did you wish to depict between them?

JH: Casting is where I get my kicks. The high is taking a risk, or you could say trusting my instinct, and not knowing exactly how it will work out. It's exciting to bring someone new to the cinema screen. I saw many people for the roles of H and D, including actors, artists, married couples, even dancers. I wanted this story to rely less on dialogue and more on body language, so I was looking at how my characters would move around the space. It was a long process but eventually I found what I was looking for. Viv had been there all along. I have known her for thirty years, but had never thought of casting her until ten days before the shoot. It was different with Liam. I knew his work as an artist but didn't know him personally. I spoke to him on the telephone and was struck by his beautiful voice.

If I'm casting non-professional actors, it's because of who they are and not because I want them to skillfully transform themselves in someone else. I may have written D in a certain way but then I look at Viv and realise I'm going to have to take on board the differences between what I've written and what is now in front of me. I have to do some letting go here and this isn't always easy, but the pay off is it's going to be a flesh and blood 'performance' that doesn't feel like a performance. And it'll be one that hasn't been seen before. This is what I find less interesting about casting well-known actors – they have been seen in a myriad of ways before and I won't be surprised.

Non-professional actors generally ask fewer questions. They can be more willing to be led and take each moment as it comes. But also I think the best actors can do this too – if they're willing to let go. This is the hardest thing. However I'm increasingly reluctant to distinguish between professional actors and non-professional actors and really it is simply a question of finding the right person for the role and less about whether they're trained or not.

JW: *Tom Hiddleston is something of a talismanic figure for you and takes a smaller but key role here. I imagine it is getting harder to afford him? How has your working relationship with Tom developed and do you take a special pride in seeing how he has conquered the acting world whilst retaining a genuine passion for his profession?*

JH: Tom will always be interested in work that challenges him. He doesn't differentiate between mainstream or independent when it comes to portraying a character. I remember when we shot *Archipelago* he would sometimes refer to Loki as someone who was also struggling to define himself within his family.

JW: *For me,* Exhibition *is a very poignant and affecting work, especially on the subject of how communication falters and breaks down between people. This is a subject to which you return often in the film, both through the use of the intercom system and the general silences and spaces in the dialogue. Is this one of the primary thrusts of the film?*

JH: I've noticed different audience reactions to H and D. Some people see them as a loving couple. Others believe the film is about the breakdown of a marriage. They think H and D are unpleasant to each other and won't stay together. I think if you've lived with someone for a long time, niceties go out of the window. Communication can be terse and abrupt but that doesn't mean the relationship is not working. We're simply not used to seeing this kind of 'reality' onscreen.

I was also interested in depicting H, the husband, as the rational and intellectual one and D as the instinctive and emotional one – but then at times contradicting this. That's life. In relationships we act out many different roles and moods.

JW: *Location is always incredibly important to your work. What was the role of the house in this instance?*

JH: My personal relationship to the space is key. It's one of the springboards for my imagination. My feelings surrounding a place become the foundations of the story.

Once I decided on this house, then so many of the visual and aural ideas followed on from there. The sponge-like nature of the house, the way it soaks in sounds from the outside so they appear to be coming from the inside. The reflections, how you can be looking out of the window and see the dining chairs floating in the garden. It was a simple matter of observing what was already there.

It became like a magic box into which I could place my dreams, memories and nightmares … I recognised from the places I have lived that homes have mood changes just like us. But maybe these mood changes can be our own projections. This house is at different times frightening, loving, possessive – it demands to be looked after. It's needy like a child.

JW: *You have always been very exacting in terms of your aesthetic but I wondered if you could talk about your approach here. You play around a lot more with both the sound design – which is very impressive – and with the editing. What were some of the meaning and emotions you wanted the spectator to experience?*

JH: Bresson's dictum 'the ear is more creative than the eye' is always ringing in my ears and I believe this wholeheartedly. As I've said before, one of the many aspects that struck me about this house was the way sounds from the street penetrated the space inside. Sometimes it was as if a noise, like a car door shutting or a voice in the street, would appear to be coming from inside. This inside/outside aspect informed the soundscape. I wanted D to imagine entire stories in her head through sound and to create the idea of a frightening world outside.

In the edit I challenged Helle and myself to make less sense and have the film work on a more unconscious level. So the connections would be more freely associated and less linear. I want to go further and further into dreams and the connections between different levels of reality, and by doing this make it possible for the audience to get inside the character's head.

Tom **Kalin**

Tom Kalin is a New York-based filmmaker, writer, producer and activist, best known as a prominent figure in the New Queer Cinema.

Kalin received a BFA in Painting (University of Illinois, 1984), an MFA in Photography and Video (Art Institute of Chicago, 1987), and completed the Independent Study Program (Whitney Museum, 1988). In addition to his feature films *Swoon* (1992) and *Savage Grace* (2007), Kalin has also created short films and video works screened in numerous international film festivals and included in the permanent collections of Centre George Pompidou, Paris and the Museum of Modern Art, New York.

Growing up next to a father who worked with juvenile delinquents, Kalin made his first feature film as an attempt to understand the so-called criminal mind, told via the story of symbolic anti-heroes. A negotiation of Kalin's particular visual style, narrative, cultural theory and social awareness, *Swoon* re-opens the notorious murder case from the 1920s in which two wealthy and educated homosexuals murdered a young boy in order to prove they were smart enough not to get caught. This famous case had already been told in two earlier films, Alfred Hitchcock's *Rope* (1948) and Richard Fleisher's *Compulsion* (1959), but Kalin was the first one not to downplay the topic of homosexuality. Richard Loeb and Nathan Leopold Jr. escaped the death penalty only because their defence was based on the argument that they were insane due to their homosexuality. With this compelling, highly stylized film, Kalin created a period picture that knows it is a period picture, deliberately deploying anachronistic props into the frame. Interested in the topic of power of sexual control, he does not depict this murder as a criminal act but as a sexual adventure that got out of hand, a murder that would never be possible without a particular psychosexual balance between the two men based on devotion and blackmail.

Initiated as a project with the producer Christine Vachon in 1992, Kalin's second feature, *Savage Grace*, was filmed fifteen years later. It is based on a true story of Barbara Daly Baekeland and her incestuous relationship with her son Anthony, responsible for murdering her in the end. A wealthy and beautiful Barbara, played by Julian Moore, is married to a successful husband and lives a perfect life. Due to excessive drinking, her marriage crumbles and Barbara desperately tries to control her homosexual son as the only man left in her life. The scenes of her decision to become a part of Anthony and his partner's sexual life opened up many questions, leaving the viewer wondering if this was a true homicide. Rather, it could be interpreted as a suicide in which the mother used her emotionally unstable son as a weapon for something she was not able to perform herself.

―――――

JASON WOOD: *How did you first come to the attention of* Savage Grace *by Natalie Robins and Steven M. L. Aronson and what particular elements attracted you to it?*

TOM KALIN: Christine Vachon gave me *Savage Grace* while I was making *Swoon* and I found the book electrifying. It's a page-turner with great sweep: a vivid mix of Greek tragedy and tabloid shocker. Primarily told in first person by participants in the Baekeland saga, its also compelling journalism with many contradictory points of view.

I was particularly haunted by Tony's description of the ruined splendour of Miramar, the house he shared with Barbara in Mallorca. I later visited it and was not disappointed. This larger-than-life true story had echoes, too, of nonfiction like Truman Capote's *In Cold Blood* [1967] or the novels of Henry James, Edith Wharton or Patricia Highsmith.

JW: *I'm sure that you are tired of people pointing them out, but there are parallels – the crime story with sexual undertones – and differences with your influential* Swoon. *Do you feel that you are drawn to flawed characters and to central relationships based on a combustible dynamic?*

TK: Between *Swoon* and *Savage Grace*, I developed two 'nonfiction' features – one about the relationship between Patti Smith and Robert Mapplethorpe and the other about an American rock band in Germany called the Monks. I wrote scripts for both but never shot them. So while absolutely, yes, there are parallels (and differences) between *Swoon* and *Savage Grace*, I am not solely interested in dark tales of fucked-up people doing terrible things to each other!

Barbara and Tony are symbiotic characters; in the mythical sense, almost two halves of one whole. So the film is grounded in both of their points of view. You could see Barbara as the main protagonist because she drives the story forward, initiates the struggle, literally. Yet her narcissistic, destructive relationship with Tony (and others) makes it difficult to identify with her.

Tony's voice-over also is a window into the film and his character offers a different emotional aspect to the story. But by the end of the film you discover that Antony is an 'unreliable narrator' that his voice-over is coming from Broadmoor.

Julianne, Eddie, Stephen – all of the actors – were brave enough not to judge their characters. I think *Savage Grace* balances a necessary distance with empathy and compassion. It seemed false to ask an audience to have catharsis or identify with them in the traditional sense.

Swoon is a much more 'romantic' movie in it's way (if that's the right way to describe it), influenced in part by couples-on-the-run films like *Badlands* [1973] or *Bonnie and Clyde* [1967]. And Nathan Leopold is clearly the protagonist of *Swoon*.

In both movies, I'm interested in characters trapped in a terrible and fatal dance. Or to use the French term, folie à deux – 'a madness shared by two'. With *Swoon*, a critic said I put the 'homo back into homicide'! In that movie I wanted to revisit film noir conventions to insist that sexual obsession could lead to murder regardless of sexual orientation. *Savage Grace* lacks that sort of didactic impetus; I really just wanted to tell the particular story of the Baekeland family as honestly as I could. It's not a 'message movie'.

With *Savage Grace* I was more interested in behaviour than 'psychology' and took wisdom from this quote by Elia Kazan: 'directing finally consists of turning psychology into behaviour'. As many have said before, film is a medium of 'show, don't tell'. I wanted to take a lyrical, visual approach to Tony and Barbara's mental breakdown and ground it in specific moments of behaviour to uncover what lays beneath the surface and make it visible.

JW: *I've always admired writer Howard Rodman. How did your collaboration unfold and how did you set about tackling the epic sweep of the literary source material and the fact that it spanned numerous decades and continents?*

TK: Howard admired *Swoon* and was very encouraging while I was writing the Smith and Mapplethorpe script. I wanted to explore working with a writer, and when I talked to him about *Savage Grace* he admitted to fear and ambivalence about the material. This seemed a useful starting point. I proposed the idea of telling this epic narrative in five days and gave him a binder of photos (from the book and other sources) and asked him to choose the key five. We were both drawn to the same photos; many of the scenes in the film spring out of these images. Though the story is literally not told in five days, the acts all show compact turning points rather than try to follow every in between moment. I also think Howard did a great job of capturing the particular locution of these rare birds, the beautifully convoluted way they speak.

JW: *How closely did you visit archive materials relating to Barbara and Tony Daly? I read in another interview that you drew particular inspiration from a photograph of Tony reclining in his bathtub. Also, were this archive materials a point of reference for your key technicians (production design, costume design and cinematography)?*

TK: The photography from the book and additional material uncovered through research were vital resources. Look in the book at the photograph taken of Barbara and Tony on the sofa in Cadogan Square – Julianne and Eddie are virtual doppelgangers. The body language, or décor, or clothing are clues to these characters and their relationships: the photographs were rich with the kind of detail that suggests a whole world. Since the film was shot entirely in and around Barcelona with a Spanish crew, it was useful for me to bring picture research about the very specific look of this social set, particularly in places like the Stork Club. We actually borrowed many props in that scene from the collection of the real Stork Club, a detail that brought it's own kind of magic. Juanmi, Victor and Gabriela – cinematographer, production designer and costume designer – were brilliant collaborators and really brought these very different periods to life. We had great fun working with colour, using it as an element in the storytelling.

JW: *Eddie Redmayne is scintillating as Antony. He captures both the impression of a character that is very uncomfortable in his own skin but also ably captures Tony's decadent decline. How did you decide upon him for the role?*

TK: I auditioned about a hundred actors for Antony. Eddie Redmayne just came in and claimed the role. He was amazing, compelling in auditions and also so beautifully simple, really just inevitable. One of the keys to Eddie's success I think is the effortless way he suggests the transition of Tony's character from the tender, carefree moments on the beach in Cadaques to the palpable doom you feel about him in London. In the small physical choices – like how he smokes a cigarette or the sweet and shy way he pulls the bed sheet up before Blanca walks in – Eddie instinctively knew how to suggest Tony's inner tensions. Eddie also has a lush, unforgettable face that evokes the 1960s. He looks very much like he could be Julianne's son too, so this adds real visceral power. You believe them on screen together.

JW: *From her work with Todd Haynes, Julianne Moore is no stranger to supporting* demanding and unconventional projects and to portraying very complex characters. Was she always your first choice for the part of Barbara?

TK: Julianne was the only actress I could imagine as Barbara. I had met her briefly while Todd Haynes was making *Safe* [1995] and *Far From Heaven* [2002]. She's very down to earth, friendly. So I wrote her a personal letter and sent the script to her, and a week later we were having lunch. She said yes right away and it's her unwavering belief and passion that really made the film possible. I showed her the pictures during that lunch and it was an uncanny added benefit how much she resembled the real person.

But it's her ability to conjure the inner life that is her gift. And this volatile, narcissist was such a very different role for Julianne, miles away from many of the things she was most known for. She has such ability to bring empathy and humanity to characters that seem almost too large for life. She makes Barbara a real, contradictory, infuriating, heartbreaking person. Julianne is amazing at finding unexpected moments of behaviour and physicality.

Without ever becoming heavy handed, Julianne and Eddie also managed to suggest one of the most mysterious tensions of this crime. I was always interested in the question while making the film: does Tony murder Barbara or is her death in some way a complicated suicide? Does she use her son as a tool with which to end her life? It's too simple to see the stabbing as a one-sided murder: there's a terrible complicity between them both at the end of the film.

JW: *Barbara has both a reckless charisma – which makes her a magnet for Brooks – but this is offset by volatility and an ultimately fatal narcissism. This comes to the fore when she insults Brooks with his new mistress at the airport. This seems to me a pivotal scene. Do you see it as one of the moments when things really begin to fall apart for her?*

TK: Yes, Barbara's private and public personas collide in the airport and her trajectory changes radically. Even though the marriage to Brooks has always been volatile, there was a certain odd balance, an unholy trinity if you will, between Barbara, Brooks and Tony before Brooks leaves. When Tony later says 'taking care of Mummy became my inheritance' or buries letters in his father's garden, you see how perilous things have become.

Her scintillating, funny, appalling monologue was a wonder to watch take after take on set. Just a complete *tour de force*. But also in small non-dialogue moments Julianne is so devastating: the way she turns around at the end of the scene and the sad, dignified way she walks away, that heartbreaking, stunned implosion. Absolutely incredible.

On set, we called that hot magenta Givenchy dress she wears in the airport the 'red menace'. Several of my collaborators who shall go unnamed doubted the choice of this amazing vintage dress. But I think it's great how she looks in those sunglasses and sling-backs, her dress just a public cry for help and explosion of rage.

JW: *There is the sense that Barbara is less troubled by Tony's homosexuality than Brooks, who seems to see it as a source of failure. Did you wish to comments on attitudes of the time or did you wish to restrict yourself to the subject in relation only to the film's central characters?*

TK: I find it too facile when people describe this as the story of a woman who sleeps with her son to cure him of his homosexuality. What transpires between Barbara and Tony is well beyond mere sex – it's about power and possession, what the book jacket describes as 'profound failure in the simplest duties of love'. I think Barbara had a complicated attitude toward her son's homosexuality and I took care in the film to not show it as simple disapproval. Brooks was much less tolerant and his attitudes were common at the time. But Barbara doesn't want anyone ultimately to come between her and Tony.

JW: *Christine Vachon has played such an important role in preserving a diversity of voices in regards to contemporary American cinema. How satisfying is it to have Christine in your corner in terms of allowing you to make the films you want to make and to make them without compromise?*

TK: Christine is just the sort of person you want with you when the boat springs a leak. We're both stubborn fighters who will sacrifice a lot for a movie we believe in. It's great to have that longevity in my career and the sense of trust and freedom that comes from years of collaboration. We also have shared an unhealthy appetite for crime writing since the first moments of our friendship.

On *Savage Grace* Christine was joined by the amazing Katie Roumel and Pamela Koffler from Killer Films. They are such a great team and have a rich trackrecord there. Killer Films put their money where their mouths are, so to speak, and have a deep belief in the value of opinionated movies.

JW: *Finally, people have commented that it has been a while since* **Swoon**. *However, in the intervening years you have not only produced films for others but have also worked in a diverse range of media. How has this work informed your more classically structured projects and what freedoms and disciplines does this experimental work afford you?*

TK: I've had an eclectic career. I've always been inspired by artists like Derek Jarman who moved so nimbly and evocatively across disciplines. I'm a restless sort, creatively. I've worked as a producer for other directors, including *Go Fish* [1994] and *I Shot Andy Warhol* [1996], and have made a diverse body of experimental film and video work alongside my narrative films for over twenty years. I love the freedom to work alone with a Super 8 camera and the formal experimentation involved in installation and single-channel work. 'Hand made' movies offer a more intimate scale and process while I develop larger feature films.

I've made a number of narrative shorts too in the past years. I collaborated with fashion designer Geoffrey Beene on a film for his thirtieth anniversary with Marcia Gay Harden, Viveca Lindfors and Claire Danes. This thirty-minute film was inspired by silent film and screened at the Whitney Museum among others. I made a short film with Frances McDormand, Lili Taylor and Will Patton, which screened on PBS in the States. And I have also taught in the graduate program at Columbia University for a decade.

Charlie **Kaufman**

The directorial debut of acclaimed writer Charlie Kaufman, whose scripts include *Being John Malkovich* (1999) and *Eternal Sunshine of the Spotless Mind* (2004), *Synecdoche, New York* (2008) is a work of rare ambition and scope.

Theatre director Caden Cotard (Philip Seymour Hoffman) is mounting a new play in Schenectady, New York but turmoil reigns as his wife has left him to pursue her painting in Berlin, taking their young daughter Olive with her. Therapy brings Caden no solace and a new relationship with the alluringly candid Hazel (Samantha Morton) has also prematurely run aground. Worried about the transience of his life, Caden heads for New York and after hiring a huge ensemble cast sets about crafting a brutally honest work that mimics his own life experiences.

Unafraid to grapple with themes of failure, disappointment and ennui, Kaufman has made a dazzlingly original film of poignancy and import. The cast is also one of the best in recent American cinema, with the outstanding Hoffman enjoying tremendous support from Michelle Williams, Hope Davis and Dianne Wiest to name but a few.

JASON WOOD: *In purely practical terms how did you find the transition from writing to directing?*

CHARLIE KAUFMAN: I always adopted the attitude with my writing that failure is not something to be avoided. I decided early on to take a similar approach with directing. I asked myself what's the worse thing that could happen here? The answer was that the movie might not come out well and that's not so terrible.

I'd always had a fairly collaborative relationship with Michel Gondry and Spike Jonze when I'd worked with them and had experience of making movies in pre-production, production and post-production stages. As well as having studied at NYU Film School I also have a theatre background and so have developed a real love of working with actors and also think that I have an intuitive feel for it. The thought of directing wasn't traumatic for me.

JW: *Synecdoche needs to be experienced numerous times. Did you make it with the intention that subsequent viewings would pay dividends?*

CK: This was absolutely my intention. I very much wanted the film to have a certain ambiguity so that you would be able to interact with it as an audience member. It allows you and encourages you to interact with it as opposed to being merely presented with a story that you simply follow. The film certainly doesn't simply give you answers and this type of cinema doesn't particularly interest me. I sometimes watch movies that do that, and find them enjoyable, but I do seek to give a more inclusive experience. I feel that theatre has a dynamism that cinema lacks and so my approach is one that hopefully embraces new discoveries. I want the film to feel fresh and different each time you watch it.

JW: *Synecdoche isn't a dream and doesn't have the same reliance on dreams as* **Eternal Sunshine of the Spotless Mind.** *It does, however, have a certain dream-like logic.*

CK: I have always been interested in dreams and am always trying to figure out what it is to me that is so powerful about dreams and to try and understand how that works. I also just think that dreams often make for really great stories. I find myself a much better storyteller in my dreams than I am when I'm awake. When you are asleep and when you are dreaming you obviously can't control your feelings and the result is often intense emotion. The idea of being confined as a storyteller to a linear, literal and fairly narrow understanding of reality is actually quite frustrating and this understanding and depiction of reality is really not of that much interest to me. There is an infinite world out there to explore.

JW: *Themes such as death, despair, loneliness and metaphysics recur. For all that though,* **Synecdoche** *still has a high comic element.*

CK: That was one of the perspectives from which I wrote it. To my mind it's funny! But I also don't want to tell people what to think and it's not my aim to say 'you should find this bit funny and that bit funny'. As we touched upon earlier it's paramount that people be allowed to have their own personal experiences of the movie. It's fine of course if they don't find any of it remotely funny but if it moves them in some other way … my feeling is that it can be both.

There is also the feeling that *Synecdoche* is pretentious because of its complexities and because of some of the language the characters use. I'm very much aware of that but this to me is also part of the fun, specifically with regards to the ways in which similar language is sometimes used in other kinds of movies. People also sometimes get nervous about laughing at things when they are in an audience in case they feel they have laughed at something inappropriate. They don't want to be embarrassed.

When we were making the film we were all very aware of this delicate balance and treated everything very seriously. This was certainly true of Philip Seymour Hoffman, who is the film's centre. In many ways it's a painful performance and his character has a lot of hurt and turmoil in him. This sense of suffering was certainly real and was felt on set by the other actors and all those working on the movie. For Philip this must have been an intense emotional experience.

JW: *Alongside Hoffman you have assembled a very impressive cast.*

CK: These are some of my all time favourite actors. I knew Catherine [Keener] quite well, but a lot of them I'd never met or worked with before. I can't tell you the feeling of having had Samantha Morton read the script and then hear that she wanted to do it; the same is true of Dianne Wiest. It was also important once I met them that we got along as people. The film was not only my first as director, it was also shot relatively quickly and so I had to ensure that everybody was going to get along as I didn't want to find myself in the position of babysitter.

JW: *You are known for writing strong female characters.* Synecdoche *features at least eight compelling women. One of the kernels of the film is Caden's inability to ever fully connect with the women in his life.*

CK: This is the big issue for Caden Cotard. In general he has a difficult time being present in any situation and because of this misses moments and opportunities. I'm not sure that I ever set out with this somewhat intellectual idea with regards to his character but it seems to be true of him. It's perhaps a human condition too.

JW: *You also present quite a challenge to Frederick Elmes. How did the veteran cinematographer respond?*

CK: It was great to work with Fred. He was passionate about the project from very early on. The biggest problem that we had was the very compact shooting schedule. We only had 45 days to shoot and so we all had to take a very pragmatic approach. Fred and I talked a lot about what we wanted the movie to feel like. We had a lot of photographs and shots of exteriors in the production office. We worked very closely on storyboarding the particularly complicated things and also spent a lot of time together with the rest of the production team finding the right locations. We also felt, and for a whole bunch of reasons but especially because aspects of the movie are so surreal and stylised, that the cinematography had to be relatively uncomplicated.

JW: *You've a good trackrecord concerning titles.*

CK: Not everyone agrees! I think *Synecdoche* has a sense of mystery to it. It has various meanings and connotations. I also just liked the way it sounded and the fact that it's a play on words to Schenectady, New York which is where the film is partly set. Believe me, I come up with a lot of titles. When people ask me why I called the film *Synecdoche* I always respond, 'Well, why not?' Besides, you might get to learn a new word.

Gideon **Koppel**

Gideon Koppel grew up in Liverpool, studied mathematics and was a postgraduate student at the Slade School of Fine Art in the Experimental Media Studio. His work is exhibited in a wide variety of forms: from the film installation for fashion label Comme des Garcons to the controversial and never broadcast BBC film *Ooh la la and the art of dressing up* which explores the psychopathology of celebrity.

Sleep Furiously (2008) became the critical discovery of the 2008 Edinburgh Film Festival, and then became one of the most critically acclaimed new British films of its year.

The film is a meditative study of a small farming community in mid-Wales which observes the rhythms of country life, and the rhythms of the monthly visits of the mobile library. But it is a life that is changing. The village school is about to close, mechanisation is replacing many of the old ways, church congregations are dwindling, but the village show and the sheepdog trials carry on. Koppel's interest in the eccentricities of life is simultaneously affectionate, moving and humorous.

JASON WOOD: *You've described the film as being influenced by conversations with the writer Peter Handke. What form did these conversations take and what were some of the primary topics?*

GIDEON KOPPEL: A few weeks into the filming of *Sleep Furiously* I was reading Peter Handke's play *Kaspar*. The world of Kaspar had a particular resonance for me at the time: exploring relationships between external and internal landscapes;

questions about belonging; a sense of what is 'possible' rather than what 'is', or 'was'; Kaspar's struggle for language, for words – his cry 'I want to be someone like somebody else once was'.

I wrote to Peter, describing the film I was making and asking if I could come to Paris to talk with him about it. One month later, over lunch we talked. We talked about all kinds of stuff, but I remember coming away thinking differently about stories – what a story could be. I really enjoyed the idea of a story as an evocation of a moment, a place in time, a gesture… But perhaps most important was Peter's response to the uncertainties I expressed about what and how I was filming. He said simply and emphatically 'follow your instinct'. Peter's words were and remain very important for me. And the conversations continue.

JW: *What is your direct relationship to the community in which you film and how did this impact upon your decision to film there and how you chose to represent it?*

GK: I guess I should start answering this question by saying that *Sleep Furiously* is not intended to be a film 'about' the community of Trefeurig – so I didn't really set out to 'represent' Trefeurig… In that sense I don't experience the film as a 'documentary', or at least what 'documentary' has become associated with now.

The writer and psychoanalyst Adam Phillips viewed two rough cuts and of the second commented that he felt there was a more developed emphasis on 'aboutness'. I enjoyed this term Adam coined and recognised my resistance to the demands for 'aboutness' and my interest in the qualities of evocation.

I wanted to make a film in which moments of intimacy and human gesture became juxtaposed with the infinite space and time of the landscape. I think about the landscape of *Sleep Furiously* as an 'internal landscape' – it has a quality of childhood about it… I suppose my own childhood, although I tried to evolve a film that touches more universal sensibilities. But it is not stuck in childhood, there is a development in the film that I perceived as a passage from nature to culture. Having said that, my relationship with the community of Trefeurig is rooted in my childhood: we used to go on family holidays there and I often 'worked' on one of the local farms with Edwin and Eleanor Hughes. I smile when I say 'work' because all I did was tag along with Mr Hughes, but it felt like work and I discovered a deep sense of contentment and satisfaction in that experience. When I was 12 or 13 my parents moved permanently from Liverpool to a smallholding in the area. Without having had any farming experience, they kept cows, sheep, goats, chickens… and I was roped into helping look after the animals. My parents, both artists and refugees, found a home and a sense of belonging in this beautiful but sometimes harsh environment. So Trefeurig became and in part remains my home too.

JW: *Before I even viewed* **Sleep Furiously** *I was immediately drawn to the title. It seems so incongruous and yet after seeing the film it seemed so apt in it's capturing an environment and a community in what has been described as 'quiet uproar'. Did you wish the title to reflect this?*

GK: This is such a difficult question because at the moment I still lack the confidence to really play with the significance of titles. It seems to me that a title is like the outline of a drawing or painting, which in turn makes me think of Marion Milner's book *On Not Being Able to Paint*. Here Milner describes 'the outline' as that which separates the external realities of the world from imaginative experience and in that sense 'the outline' becomes the containment of what might otherwise be an unmanageable madness. I suppose what I am saying is that for me the title can generate boundaries in which the film evolves as an autonomous world with its own logic, moralities… *Sleep Furiously* had a working title of *The Library Van*, which I liked for its direct simplicity. For me this title suggested the possibilities of the van as an actual and metaphoric vehicle of stories, but I feared it might reinforce the film being perceived as a documentary 'about' a library van.

I used the cutting room as I would a studio space – covering the walls with images and text. My eyes, my mind could wander away from the screen I was working on to these associative elements I had found throughout the making process. One of these elements was a large graphic of the Chomsky phrase 'colourless green ideas sleep furiously'. At one point I removed this sheet from the wall and paced it directly under my monitor. In this act 'sleep furiously' became the title of the film. I don't really want to explain my thinking about the title beyond that point.

JW: *Acting as your own cinematographer you preference long, unhurried takes, with your camera remaining static as it observes life passing in and out of the frame. What was the defining principle behind this aesthetic choice?*

GK: When I composed pictures in the viewfinder I was thinking about using the frame to create a stage. In that sense, every environment becomes a theatrical set in which a drama could – no 'would' – take place … a story would unfold. This space within a frame also offered a containment of time, rhythm and ritual – three dynamics that are very important for me – perhaps the essential components of stories.

The camera becomes a microscope through which I can explore the world – in doing so everything I observe becomes, to different degrees, fictionalised. What do I mean by that? Well I guess that the composition suggests relationships between objects that are not otherwise there. Imagine looking out over the

Sleep Furiously, Gideon Koppel, 2008 (New Wave)

valley, the fields, fences, house… the sheep and the trees are just a part of that continuum. But through the camera, they can be brought together – perhaps it is the lens making the tree and the sheep appear to be on the same focal plane, or they are isolated, contained within the frame as in a way to highlight their presence above all the other stuff in view. Either way, there is now a suggestion that the sheep and tree are in some sort of communion.

Perhaps this might be saying the obvious, but *Sleep Furiously* is a fairly accurate translation of how I see and experience the world. That is to say the images on screen are very close to the images of my mind's eye – a quality of contemplation and gaze that, to my great frustration, did not help my childhood ambitions to be a good goalkeeper.

JW: *It is perhaps unavoidable that some moments in* **Sleep Furiously** *evoke a bygone era but the film, because of the issues it seeks to address, never settles for mere nostalgia. Was this, and overtures towards sentiment, something that you were keen to avoid?*

GK: Almost every story in *Sleep Furiously* suggests both beginning and ending – the circularity of life. The owl dies but then becomes something else – a sculpture; the piglets are cute and loveable but will be equally appealing when unrecognisable – grilled with a little salt and pepper.

I guess that the paradoxical and contradictory in life, however difficult, are important for me. So it is not that I set out to specifically eliminate sentimentality or nostalgia; my intention was for the film to create its own moral constructs rather than use assumed values.

JW: *It strikes me that sound as well as image is particularly important to you. This is a film that I could imagine experiencing with my eyes closed. I would still take enjoyment and enlightenment from it. Was sound design something to which you paid particular attention?*

GK: I trained for three years as a sound recording engineer at Utopia Studios in London, working on all kinds of music projects from the Queen soundtrack for the feature film *Flash Gordon* [1980] to *Neutronica*, an album by Donovan. It is funny but I wasn't interested in the music bit at all, but was really curious about sounds and used studio 'downtime' to make sound montages. That later developed into a fascination with the juxtaposition of sound and picture. Jean-Luc Godard's *Prénom Carmen* [1983] and *Passion* [1982] had a big impact. I thought it was magical to be immersed in an image of the sea at nighttime while hearing the sound of a train... then propelled into an acute sense of the infinite as the sound of the train was suddenly replaced by the distant waves...

I think about the microphone like I do the camera – as a kind of microscope on the world. Not merely to record sounds that accompany or illustrate the image, but to create another dimension to the picture.

JW: *I wondered also if you could talk about Aphex Twin.*

GK: It isn't an original score. It is made from existing Aphex Twin tracks, so in that sense there wasn't a collaboration with Richard James. This music naturally found its way into the film from very early on in the editing process. It is not an accompaniment, but becomes a form of voice for the each of the main characters. I sent Richard a DVD of a rough edit of *Sleep Furiously* – he really liked the film but was irritated by the way I had edited the music: cutting tracks short, repeating sections... we were both sorry that there wasn't time for him to compose a specific soundtrack. The music is such a vital part of the film – I am really grateful to Richard for his generosity and support.

JW: *Do you see the film as existing in any sort of documentary tradition? Serge Lalou [Être et Avoir, 2002] is an associate producer and Raymond Depardon also comes to mind. Interestingly, Mark Cousins who has been a passionate supporter, located* Sleep Furiously *in the tradition of Humphrey Jennings. Elsewhere, the film's psychogeographical bent has evoked Chris Petit and Andrew Kötting.*

GK: Mark Cousins provoked me to look again at the work of Humphrey Jennings and also introduced me to an wonderful film – *Farrebique* (1946) by Georges Rouquier. Another writer on film, Neil Young, equated *Sleep Furiously* with the work of James Benning. I hadn't heard of Benning, so eagerly went to see *RR* [2007] at the BFI Southbank. What a revelation. It is one the most powerful pieces of cinema I have seen for years.

I guess that with Serge's involvement, the comparisons with *Être et Avoir* are inevitable, but the Philibert film which has a resonance for me is *La Ville Louvre* [1990], Kötting's *Gallivant* [1996] and above all Chris Marker's *Sans Soleil* [1983] are all contemporary 'documentaries' that are important to me. But as to *Sleep Furiously* existing in a documentary tradition? It seems to me that since the 1920s filmmakers and artists from Vertov to Chris Marker have used notions of 'documentary' as a way of qualifying work that did not have a screenplay scripts, that are open ended … what might be called ciné poems. I use the word 'documentary' cautiously because unfortunately what was once an idiom of filmmaking and art is now often conflated by both broadcasters and academics with factual television programme production. That is to say, polemical themes and journalistic structures prevail over visual observations and lyrical stories. The camera is used more as a recording device, than a kind of microscope that contains, discovers and evokes dynamics of the world that otherwise pass by unnoticed.

Harmony **Korine**

After spending much of his youth in Nashville, Tennessee, Harmony Korine moved to New York aged 18 and studied English at New York University for one semester before dropping out. During this time, in which he was living in his grandmother's basement in Queens, he met photographer Larry Clark, and wrote the screenplay for *Kids* (1995). A provocative tale of teenage sex, the film became one of the most provocative works of its decade.

Korine made his directorial debut with the equally controversial *Gummo* in 1997. Featuring the return to the screen of Linda Manz, the film is set around the impoverished residents of Xenia, Ohio. Featuring incredibly naturalistic performances from its young cast, the film presents an authentic look at blue-collar life and poverty-line existence. Realism and poetry effortlessly mesh.

The first American work to be certified by the filmmaking collective Dogme 95, Korine's *Julien donkey-boy* (1999) confirmed the director as one of the most unique voices in contemporary American cinema. The story of the schizophrenic Julien (Ewan Bremner in a role partly based on Korine's own uncle), his pregnant sister Pearl (Chloë Sevigny) and their maniacal father (a terrific Werner Herzog, who would remain a recurring figure in Korine's life), the film is an intelligent observation of life on the margins.

Filmed in Panama, Scotland and France, *Mister Lonely* (2007) is another tale of misfits, this time a group of impersonators, amongst them Samantha Morton, Diego Luna and Denis Lavant who form their own little community. Premiered in Cannes, the film had less of an impact that Korine's previous work and the director withdrew into other disciplines, including a collection of short stories and various other art projects.

Emerging again in 2013, Korine delivered his least divisive and most commercially successful work to date with *Spring Breakers*. A look at the spring break

Spring Breakers, Harmony Korine, 2013 (Chris Hanley/Muse Film)

tradition in the United States, it's a neon-infused tale of crime, sisterhood and debauchery.

JASON WOOD: *You have said that the starting point for* Spring Breakers *was an image of girls in bikinis with guns.*

HARMONY KORINE: I had been collecting spring break imagery for a while, mainly for art projects and paintings. I started to look at all the imagery together and that world with its hyper-sexual and hyper-violent subject matter. There were also all these pop kind of details and pop culture indicators such as nail varnish, dunkin' donuts boxes, puke and they just spoke to me. I started to dream things up such as girls on the beach in bikinis with guns robbing fat tourists. These images were striking and they stayed with me. From there I came up with a storyline.

JW: *And you wrote in Florida during an actual spring break.*

HK: I did. I found a human jawbone in a chandelier at a Days Inn hotel and I decided to stay there and write the script. This was in Panama City during spring break two years ago.

JW: *Is the spring break as debauched as you depict it?*

HK: It's a common thing in America. I grew up around it. It happens once a year. Kids go off, cut loose, destroy everything and then go home as if it didn't happen. At the same time I didn't want to make a movie that was an expose of spring break. It's a pop poem, an impressionistic reinterpretation of those things. It's pushed into something more imaginary. What happens in the film is far removed from what actually happens on a spring break.

JW: *From* Gummo *onwards, location has always been a key facet of your work. It functions almost as a character.*

HK: I have always been obsessed with tones and feeling in films and I wanted this move to be a kind of post-articulation in the way that it was more inexplicable and like a drug experience. It had to have a transcendence, reaching a peak before disappearing into black. Much of this has to do with the feel of the locations and the ambience of the film. I have said that this film is about the culture of surfaces and the way things look. There is a candy-coated reality and all the pathology and menace and the violence is the residue of this. I wanted the film to look like it was lit with skittles. I wanted you to be able to taste it. Location is a big part of this process. I like to go down on my own a couple of months earlier and get lost. I don't ask any questions, I just drive around and this is how I happen across quite a lot of my locations.

JW: *The stardom and profile of the cast must have made for a difficult shoot in terms of public interest.*

HK: It was crazy. There was stuff I had never had to deal with before. The chaos that follows these girls is insane. I certainly wasn't used to it. It was a challenge. We were shooting in real locations and the crew was relatively small and so a lot of the energy in the film actually came from being chased. There were times when crowds would start to line up and vastly outnumber the crewmembers. Selena had one or two difficult moments where the crowds made it hard for her to concentrate but the actors were really bold and totally went for it.

JW: *How much pleasure did you take from subverting their personas?*

HK: It was a lot of fun. I enjoyed it.

JW: *James Franco is something else. How much did he bring to the character of Alien?*

HK: He is a maniac. He attacks life. Culture has become so corporate and generic and even the actors that people think of as outspoken are usually lame. Culture seems to be run by accountants and actors have themselves become accountants. Franco refuses to exist in that way. He invents things as he goes along which is something I understand. I always admired him as an actor and he had liked my movies so we had spoken about doing something together. He's a handsome man so gets leading man parts but I always thought of him as more of a character actor and his tendency in his personal life is to be adventurous and extreme and risky and so I wanted to do something where he could push that aspect of himself.

The Alien character was based on kids I used to ride the bus to school with. They would just rap. They would end up coming into school with guns and I always wondered what would happen to these kids if they didn't die by the age of thirty? I thought they would become just like Alien. I called Franco up and described the part. I also did something that I never do and spoke to him before I had written the script to make sure that it might be something that he was interested in. He immediately said 'Yes'. I then went at it. I didn't want him to be just one thing. I wanted him to be like a gangster mystic. He is a sociopath but he is also a poet and a clown. I wanted to exude a charisma and represent some strange kind of cultural mash up. For the year prior to the film I would send Franco YouTube clips and audio clips of rappers and video clips of girls getting into fights in parking lots at three in the morning. Things that I felt spiritually pertained to his character and would shape his worldview. Franco never responded. Every now and then I would get a message back saying something like 'Peace' and I was like, what does that even mean? Is he even watching this shit?

About a month before shooting he came down and didn't want to rehearse. We would just drive around St. Petersburg at 2am and he would sit in the back with his windows rolled down and I would say things like 'That's the house you cooked crack in when you were twelve. That's the broadwalk where you robbed your first tourist. This is the school you got expelled from and here is the playground where you used to get beat up as a kid.' That was it. He would just quietly breathe it all in. On the day of shooting I was nervous but really hoping he would pull it off. We put him in his costume and he just walked out and he had obviously been consuming it all and taking it in the whole time. I was like, 'holy shit'. I was blown away.

JW: *How did you cast Gucci?*

HK: He is one of my favourite rappers. He's the rap Frank Sinatra. I had always wanted to do something with him so I called up his manager but found out he was in jail. I managed to talk to Gucci in jail and told him that I had a party waiting for him when he got out of jail. He got out and did it. He's back in jail now. It sucks.

JW: *What about the twins?*

HK: The twins are my friends. They are scumbags. But they are amazing scumbags. They are what make America great. They live with no filter. Their philosophy boils down to the idea of double penetration. They exist only to double penetrate. They don't drink water. They exist on Vicodin and Redbull and piss kidney stones all day long.

JW: *I am an admirer of Benoît Debie who also shot* Calvaire *[2004]*, Innocence *[2004] and* Enter the Void *[2009].*

HK: He's an amazing cinematographer. He really is one of the best. I wanted the film to have this kind of liquid narrative and to work in a way that is perhaps closer to electronic or loop-based music. I am a friend of Noe and I had always talked to him about working with Benoît who is really super inventive, especially when it comes to colour. It is like he is making paintings. He is also completely fearless.

JW: *There is a lovely use of repetition in the film. It reminded me of listening to a catchy pop song. It's not something we've seen from you before.*

HK: It's something I have been trying to develop for a while, the notion of film as a physical experience, as something inexplicable. There is a false notion that I am obsessed with truth in cinema. I don't care about truth in cinema and never have. I think that truth is boring for the most part and what I am trying to create is something more energy-based, a kind of energy. I wanted to give the sense that the image had exploded and that energy and sounds were flooding in from all directions. I didn't know if it would work in a feature but I had been playing around with this idea in some of my shorts. I had also tried it in some of the advertising assignments that I do every once in a while. With pop music the repeated audio hooks become like mantras and this really fascinated me. Some of the lines can be very simple and base, but after they are repeated they are in some way elevated.

JW: *The music is a good combination of Cliff Martinez, Soderbergh's regular collaborator, and Skrillex.*

HK: Again, I was looking for a special kind of energy. I wanted the sound to be bombastic and at the same time beautiful. I wanted there to be an invisible line where sound design and music become one and the same. I wanted it to be very physical. As a kid I used to live in an area where kids would have these huge boom boxes just playing bass and it was like bombs going off. I wanted that rattle; I wanted that thing in your gut. I wanted it to rattle the fuck out of you.

JW: *You obviously had a very specific sense of how* Spring Breakers *should look and feel. Chris Cunningham's* Window Licker *comes to mind for me.*

HK: In the old days I would watch movies compulsively before I would go out and make a movie. Now, I watch less and less. About a year before I start shooting I tune them out. Films obviously mean a lot to me but I never try to consciously reference other works, not just films but other art works. The stuff that has really influenced me has manifested inside, it just kind of lives there so I don't feel the need to consciously reference it. I prefer now to let myself dream and develop my own ideas. The only thing I did watch a lot before was Michael Mann's *Miami Vice* [2006]. I would watch it with the sound off. I love the way Florida looks in that film.

JW: *You avoid offering any overt moral views on the actions of the characters in this film.*

HK: I don't like to invent characters and then condemn them. That's not to say that there isn't condemnation present in the film but I don't necessarily feel I have to punish people for doing things, at least not in an obvious way. In life I have noticed that good people do terrible things and that terrible people also do good things and what's to say that these people won't eventually be punished, in the case of this movie, five seconds after the movie is over. I hate it when people get arrested and go to jail. I'm sure it will probably happen but I don't want to waste time showing that. I want things to exist in a way that allows you to dream it up yourself.

JW: *What do you feel are the processes that you have gone through with* Kids, Gummo, Julien donkey-boy, Mister Lonely *and* Trash Humpers *to get you to this point?*

HK: I feel like I can do anything. Nothing can ever stop me. I am fortified and on the side of righteousness. I am a soldier of cinema.

Andrew **Kötting**

I can't improve on the director's own biography, which appears at the foot of this book's preface, so won't try.

Despite not wishing to assert any personal familiarity with the figures in this book, Andrew Kötting is someone whose work I have long admired and a figure with whom I have become familiar over the years. He is much like his films; restless, passionate, voracious and endlessly inquisitive.

An idiosyncratic and in many ways visionary filmmaker, my bond with Kötting and his work was further cemented when my company released *Ivul*. Set in the French Pyrenees, the film is an intriguing family drama in which the intense relationship between teenage siblings Alex and Freya incurs the rage of their authoritarian father.

After a huge quarrel, Alex climbs onto the roof of the house and vows never again to set foot on the earth.

Inspired by his childhood memories, Kötting's most linear work to date is an intoxicating and ambitious combination of narrative, magical realism and vertiginous performance art.

―――――

JASON WOOD: *There's been a long hiatus between* This Filthy Earth *and* Ivul.

ANDREW KÖTTING: It's par for the course I guess with the kind of work that I make. *Gallivant* came out and did relatively well and certainly got a lot of people very interested in it after it's initial screening at Edinburgh. Even when I was making *This Filthy Earth* the idea behind *Ivul* certainly existed but I didn't really know what

Ivul, Andrew Kötting, 2009 (Sciapode/Artificial Eye)

form I wanted it to take. John Cheetham, Andrew Mitchell and I wrote the first drafts together and the BBC committed to that but then it went into a vault whille they developed their digital channels. Then *This Filthy Earth* came out and I think people thought 'Do we really want another one of those?' For me this was quite reassuring and there was a slight sense of relief that I wouldn't have to make it and I could get on with some of the other stuff that I wanted to do. Then three years ago E. D. Distribution who distribute my work in France were approached by a young producer, Émilie Blézat who expressed an interest in producing the film after reading the script and falling madly in love with it. Various meetings took place in Paris and the French Pyrenees – an area I know well – and suddenly the project took on a new life. The catch of course was that I had to translate the script into French and transpose it to a completely different landscape.

JW: *You are amongst a recent group of British filmmakers, including Ben Hopkins and Thomas Clay, who, having found it difficult to get their work financed in the UK, have relocated abroad. How did shooting outside of the UK in the French Pyrenees feed into the sensibility of the film?*

AK: I love language and I love to play with it. I have a massive archive – both sonic and visual – that helps. Inevitably, elements from my archive find their way into my work, whether it is in the films or the other media pieces. The nuance of French still escapes me, which means that I tended to simplify things and not get too complicated. I kept the story and the images simpler and made a point, not something I often do, of telling a story. I think people are more forgiving of *Ivul* because it is in French. I have a feeling that people were less forgiving of *This Filthy Earth* because it was located in the Yorkshire Dales and people spoke the mother tongue. Because *Ivul* takes place in France people seem to be attributing to it a kind of fairytale element.

JW: *Landscape is tremendously central to your work, which often attempts a dialogue with your environments.*

AK: Every film I have ever made from *Klipperty Klop* [1984] onwards has involved my confronting the landscape in some way. I love the idea of getting my hands dirty and even allowing elements such as rain to come into the lens. For me its very corporeal and I like to convey that in the very fabric of the film, which is why the work is sometimes bizarre and has strange rhythms.

JW: Ivul *is dedicated to your mother who you credit with keeping the family together. The notion of family is another central element of your work. It was the core of the recent* In the Wake of a Deadad *project, for example.*

AK: I draw on my life for inspiration and feed that back into my work. *In the Wake of a Deadad* was an exorcism in many ways. The father in *Ivul* is the kind of dad I wished I'd had; eccentric and strange and loveable. My mother, like many others of that generation, really did hold the family together and had to make tremendous sacrifices to do so. Even as an adolescent growing up I would be astonished at what she would do to keep us as a unit. Marie, the mother in the film, is obviously very different to my mother and she reaches a moment where she has simply had enough. My mother never reached that moment.

JW: *Jacob Auzanneau is remarkable as Alex. It's less a performance, more a performance piece.*

AK: He was actually much less intimidated by the physical acts he had to perform, many of which were filmed the winter before we actually started official production on the film, and more fearful of having to act. He was only sixteen when he came down to the Pyrenees to climb trees and it was just a tiny crew working with him at this time. The following summer, when the money came through and work on the film proper began, the thought of having to scale houses didn't worry him at all as he is a trained acrobat who has worked with the likes of Cirque de Soleil. It was the acting that worried him. What I tried to communicate to him, and something I carry with me through all the films, is that it is only a film. Of equal importance to everyone involved is the journey of making it. I am not in thrall to the hierarchy of cinema and make sure I communicate this to my actors. They are free to improvise and act spontaneously and often it is these unguarded and unscripted moments that become central in my films.

JW: *We earlier referred to the fact that you work across various disciplines and allow these various practices to feed into each other.* Ivul *contains experimental elements, from the archive footage and the various sonic experiments, but I was impressed by your relative restraint here.*

AK: There was a lot of pressure on me in the post-production stage and this was the first time that I was subjected to test audience screenings. It was also done very much in a collaborative spirit, both with the actors and technicians and the producers and financiers. I also did put a certain amount of pressure on myself with regards to making sure that I actually told a story. *Ivul* is all about telling a story, creating tension and making sure that it's sharp.

JW: *What kind of influences did you draw upon?*

AK: *The Moon and the Sledgehammer* [1971] by Philip Trevelyan is a key text for me and I used the film as a companion piece when making *Ivul*. I made sure that I showed it to everyone working on the film, especially the two cameramen, Gary Parker and Nick Gordon Smith and looked to them to capture that film's sense of spontaneity. Ben Rivers is another filmmaker who does something similar and there are probably elements of Ben's work in *Ivul*. In a more purely visual sense I am drawn to Matthew Barney's work. You can almost smell and taste his films. Herzog is another filmmaker who is always in the back of my mind. Herzog is so primal.

JW: Ivul *is actually part of a planned trilogy.*

AK: That's right. *This Filthy Earth* was the first. That film was set on the ground, *Ivul* is obviously partly set above the ground and the third part of the trilogy will take place underground. Xavier Tchili who plays Lek will arrive underground and meander through the underworld. There are some beautiful cave structures I have been exploring in France, Cornwall and the Faroe Islands. Xavier is a classically trained actor and of course in *Ivul* he doesn't get to speak. I've promised in that when he arrives in the underworld he'll have dialogue. The intention is that he'll meet some of the characters from the other two films. There's no script as yet, just ideas and a landscape.

Joe **Lawlor** and Christine **Molloy**

Over the past four years Christine Molloy and Joe Lawlor have been working on a project called *Civic Life*. It involves local community groups in the production of nine high-quality short films for the cinema, shot on 35mm Cinemascope and making extensive use of long takes. In 2004, their film *Who Killed Brown Owl* won the award for Best British Short Film at the Edinburgh International Film Festival. In January 2008 their latest short film *Joy* won the Prix UIP Rotterdam at the International Film Festival Rotterdam. *Helen* (2008), the first feature of the duo, who work under the title of Desperate Optimists, marks the culmination of the *Civic Life* series.

An expansion of *Joy*, *Helen* is an hypnotic first feature and marks an exciting discovery for British arthouse cinema. An 18-year-old girl named Joy has gone missing. A college-mate a few weeks away from leaving her care home, Helen, is asked to 'play' Joy in a police reconstruction that will retrace Joy's last known movements. Joy represents all that was missing from Helen's life – she had parents, a boyfriend, a future. Gradually Helen immerses herself in the role, and by borrowing elements of Joy's life begins herself to bloom.

Remarkable for its examination of identity and representation, *Helen* is also marked by its casting from within the community in which it was set and its incredibly epic visual aesthetic and use of Cinemascope.

Desperate Optimists have recently completed their second feature, the Singapore-set *Mister John* (2013), which features Aiden Gillen as a man seeking the truth behind his brother's death.

JASON WOOD: *How did Desperate Optimists and your initial work in community theatre and experimental performance begin?*

CHRISTINE MOLLOY AND JOE LAWLOR: We both started to work together, in what can broadly be described as community arts, back in the mid-1980s in Dublin. Initially the kinds of projects we ran were not art-form led, but instead we allowed the interests of the given community groups we were working with to suggest the art form required. So for example, some projects required writing to be the focus, others were more visual arts orientated and some navigated towards the theatre. The side effect of this is that we developed a very eclectic way of working before finally specialising in writing and theatre. However, we guess the art form that has inspired us the most has always been cinema. To our shame, long periods of time can go by now without us ever going to the theatre but we watch films pretty much on a daily basis.

JW: *How did this interest in cinema evolve to encompass the production of short films and how was this production informed by other disciplines?*

CM/JL: Because we did not specialise early on in our various community projects, but instead kept things very open and fluid, we thought nothing of having live or pre-recorded film and video on stage in our subsequent theatre work. We liked very much sharing the stage with these other art forms and technologies in our live performances. They were a lot of fun to work with in creating more complex and layered approaches to narrative, performance and time. The audience reactions were not always much fun. We made very challenging theatre; maybe too much so. We noticed, however, that the more we worked with film and video the more we enjoyed the filmmaking process. We recall on one of our last theatre shows that the moving image component was around fifty per cent of the live experience. We calculated that it wouldn't be long before our theatre work would be a hundred per cent moving image and none live and that this could be a real problem for a paying public intent on seeing a live production. The writing was on the wall in that sense and it was an easy decision to make to stop live theatre work and concentrate on the thing that made us happiest.

In the late 1990s when we began to move from theatre into moving image the practical reality of limited access to expensive technology and lack of money directed us to internet moving image projects to begin with before we progressed to video works and finally to short films on 35mm for cinema. One of the things about this progression is that we were always interested in what was formally possible in the medium we were working in. This clearly carries its responsibilities but we also enjoyed pushing the boundaries. Cinema, for reasons perhaps beyond the scope of this response, is a form that is quite conservative and one you have to be careful with in terms of how you push the form. That said, we love cinema driven by a formal bravery.

JW: *The notion of community has been a constant thread. Why is this notion so essential to you and what benefits have you found to have arisen from working in what can be considered a grass roots fashion?*

CM/JL: Even though we have been working on and off with various community groups for over twenty years it is only in the last six years, while working on our *Civic Life* project, that something of a certain clarity has begun to emerge. There's no doubt that much of the impetus for our work as been a certain social and political commitment. At the same time we are fascinated by the interplay of seemingly contradictory processes that underpin our *Civic Life* films. So, on the one hand, we very deliberately strive for the high production values of big budget mainstream Hollywood films by making use of 35mm Cinemascope, anamorphic lenses, elaborate and technically complicated crane shots (or steadicam shots) and highly choreographed long takes. While on the other hand we use ordinary, real people from the community – non-professionals – who we then immerse in this stylised cinematic world. What emerges is a sort of authenticity that arises from the rawness of the performances counteracted by the slickness of the production values.

We like tension and it is this that has drawn us to working with community groups on these films. The flawed, imperfect nature of the films, we hope, are the very qualities that open up a space for the audience. It is this 'space' that we try to create when making the films – a space in which accidents might happen and in which things might come alive. We see *Helen* as a sort of high point in all of this but the film also exposes some potential limitations in the *Civic Life* method. We have a growing sense that it's possible *Helen* may represent the end of a way of working for us. This might need explaining. In very crude terms *Helen* has allowed us to imagine our next feature film and because of the ambitions we have for it we are aware that these ambitions may not be best served using the *Civic Life* approach. Some of the methods we have honed and explored over the past five years may have to be attenuated but this is something we are ready for, as we believe that with *Helen* we have probably pushed the *Civic Life* project as far as it can go.

JW: *How did* Who Killed Brown Owl, *the first film in the* Civic Life *series come about and what decisions shaped your aesthetic approach and distinct take on narrative?*

CM/JL: The commission came from Enfield Council. Rather than spending the money on fireworks – which was very much an option – Enfield Council wanted to commission a film project to celebrate the successful completion of the Council's New River Loop Restoration Project. It was our desire to involve as many local people as possible in the project and to this end we held a number of civic meetings and ran a stall at a local summer fete in an attempt to drum up local involvement. Mindful that we wanted to avoid the pitfall of producing a Tourist Board film, we were nonetheless convinced we should strive for something painterly, beautiful and elegant to match the setting itself. Although we did undercut this Arcadian fantasy by lacing the film with some murder, mayhem and dysfunction.

Instinctively we knew that video would never deliver the film that we wanted to produce but we had no idea, never having worked with film before, if the budget of £20,000 would cover the dramatically cinematic ambitions we were beginning to develop, particularly knowing that we also wanted to output to film. There were two things that became clear to us very early on. Firstly, in order for the production budget to work we would only be able to afford the equipment and crew for one day. Secondly, in order for the post-production budget to work we would only be able to develop a minimal quantity of stock.

The logistical constraints demanded by the limited budget began to force a set of aesthetic decisions on us that very much fell into line with our own desires about how we might 'stage' the film event itself and develop strategies for working with a cast of non-professionals. It became clear very quickly that the 'long take' would provide us with the solution we required and it is this use of the long take, coupled with the challenge of working with non-professional actors and minimal rehearsal time, that has resulted in the distinctive approach to narrative and performance to have emerged from the *Civic Life* series of films. One way or another, given our background in experimental performance in which the 'liveness' of the event was always foregrounded, we're convinced we would have been drawn to the long take and what it offered up to us as short filmmakers desiring to experiment in cinematic time and space.

JW: *How did you find the transition from shorter pieces to feature-length work?*

CM/JL: To date we have made nine *Civic Life* short films. All of these have been made using more or less the same rules. We use long takes, we work with mainly non-professional casts from the local community, we shoot 35mm Cinemascope using anamorphic lenses and we output to film, preferably premiering in a local multiplex cinema. Over these five years we have certainly discovered the parameters of what is possible working in this way.

After the success of *Who Killed Brown Owl* we decided we wanted to make a series of films using this methodology and we randomly came up with the idea of seven short films. It was never our intention to aim towards a feature-length film. It was only after we'd completed the final film in the series and were receiving invitations from festivals to screen all seven films together that the idea of a *Civic Life* feature film began to take hold.

A well-funded commission from the Liverpool Biennial and the Liverpool Culture Company allowed us to experiment with making a longer *Civic Life* film. The resulting half-hour film, *Daydream*, was shot over four days and provided us with a very tough learning curve. A beautiful but deeply flawed film – a noble failure we hope – *Daydream* provided us with the key to plan our approach to the shooting of a feature film. Indeed, if we hadn't made *Daydream* we're convinced *Helen* would have been a disaster. We learnt that we would have to free ourselves from a strict adherence to the *Civic Life* rules and explore a more flexible approach to the use of the long take to ensure that we would have options at the editing stage. The realities of working with such a perilously low shooting ratio of only 1:3 and having only 30,000 feet of film (equivalent to only 300 mins of exposed film in the can) from which to extract a 79-minute feature film meant we had to come up with some new strategies. At the end of the day, this was always going to be the challenge of translating the *Civic Life* method from a short film to a feature-length film – the need to develop the narrative over time.

The long take has always allowed us a tremendous sense of flexibility, enabling us to react on the day regardless of the many variables thrown up by our methodology. For a feature film – that is ultimately dramatic in its structure – by its very nature, more has to be pinned down and no matter how loose, fluid and open we might want to keep things as we are filming, the narrative structure has to work. Understanding how we might use cutaways and sequences that were freed up from serving the demands of the narrative – like the sequences in the woods – was central to making the transition to a feature-length film.

JW: *Environment is also essential to you. How did you utilise your local environment in* **Helen** *and how did you seek to replicate this environment on screen?*

CM/JL: As a precondition to how the financing works on these *Civic Life* films, the commissioning organisation often has strong feelings about *where* the film should be located. For example, Birmingham was very much interested in us filming not just in their city but also specifically in Handsworth Park itself. Now, to some this might sound like a real constraint but we find it helpful to have these strictures. Our analogy is something like a jazz structure. The stronger the structure that Miles Davis lays down the easier it will be for John Coltrane to find the freedom to play. If there's no structure you end up spending all your time looking for it. So, by narrowing down the locations we can work in, you begin (subconsciously) to work with some parameters. So in effect, the starting points for all these films are, as the question suggests, environments, locations and sites. These become central to everything.

Mister John, Joe Lawlor and Christine Molloy, 2013 (Desperate Optimists/Artificial Eye)

Many years ago we used to go through writing exercises. A thorny issue for writers is starting points. How does one start? Over the years this question has become quite abstract for us, as it seems very simple. Yes, it could be a location like a park or a building for that matter. One phrase that came up many years ago was a Williams Carlos Williams quote: 'In things not in ideas.' Location seems a perfect place from which to build narratives. In fact they are perfectly suited to cinema. We'll come back to the question of how we seek to replicate this environment on screen further down the line.

JW: *I imagine that you also cast from within the local community. If so, this tactic pays particular dividends in the performance of Annie Townsend as the eponymous college girl whose upbringing is in contrast to the missing person she is asked to replicate.*

CM/JL: Our cast for *Helen* came entirely from within the local community. As with all our *Civic Life* films, by and large, whoever turns up on the day is in the film. The exception to this is how we cast the title role of Helen. We knew it would be impossible without a more traditional approach to the casting process. We couldn't just take the first young woman that came our way and give her the part. In fact, in the end, we really struggled to get anyone even close to what we needed and time was very quickly running out. With only two weeks to go before we were due to begin shooting our film we still hadn't found our lead performer.

In the end it came down to two young women. We were getting nervous, come early October, so much so that we actually approached the agent of a very talented rising star from Dublin and asked if we could arrange an audition. It went against all our desires to consider a professional, experienced actress for the part but our back was very much up against the wall. We liked this young woman very much and might have cast her there and then if we didn't have the tough skin that many years hanging from the cliff ledge has given us. We went back to our funders to look for their help and the Newcastle/Gateshead Initiative put us in contact with Open Clasp, a local women's group. Annie Townsend came to an audition we arranged with Open Clasp.

We specifically recall taking Annie's photo and she had a very strong way about her as she was photographed which impressed us. She appears vulnerable but there's an incredible strength there. She also seemed to have a very clear and strong sense of how she wanted to be presented which wasn't about what she thought we might want from her. We felt she had a very quiet and restrained but compelling presence on film. The Irish actress would have brought a lot of experience to the shoot as opposed to Annie's complete lack of experience but it was this quality, this rawness that we loved in the end. We don't like to over direct so we pretty much wanted to let Annie interpret the role the way she felt it should be done. It was an act of faith that we believe paid off in the end. Annie will have to take all the credit for her wonderful performance though. She very much led the way and set the tone.

JW: *You err towards understatement and precision.*

CM/JL: We're not sure exactly why we have arrived at such a particular way of filming and framing scenes (this may answer your earlier point about how we replicate environments and locations on the screen) but we suspect we like to keep the actual technical aspects of what we do very simple. For example, if there is a scene between people in a domestic place we always try to work out the best way to film that scene and leave it at that. The idea of breaking down the shot doesn't come very naturally to us and to be honest feels like a very tedious task. Filming the same scene from a variety of angles fills us with dread. When we've done it, it feels very mechanical and not something that we find interesting.

Now this might sound like we're slackers but in reality we very much like cinema which has a certain theatricality to it and one formal approach that can draw out this theatrical quality is to keep the cutting down to a minimum. Of course, if you are going to be so minimal with your shot list you have to very careful and clear about how you are going to set about the task. Perhaps this is where the sense of precision comes in. But in reality it's probably just the perception of precision as we don't imagine our methodology is any more precise than someone who likes very fast cutting.

Oddly, when we were filming *Helen* we sensed in some of the crew a restlessness. It was almost as if they wanted the shooting schedule to be very fast and physically demanding with lots of set ups and location changes. The idea that we might have just one or two set ups in the entire day was perplexing to them. Perhaps there is such a thing as arthouse crews, rom-com crews, action crews…

JW: *In a film that is so beautifully calibrated, it seems unfair to single individuals out for praise but Dennis McNulty's ambient score cannot pass without mention and I can't imagine the film without it. Had you worked with McNulty before and what was his brief on this project?*

CM/JL: Dennis did a great job. We have known him for several years since we were commissioned to represent Ireland at the Bienal de São Paulo in 2004 where we got on very well. So there were no doubts we could all work together. We approached music for *Helen* in a cautious way. We asked Dennis to compose music for our short film *Joy*, a companion piece to *Helen*, and agreed that if this went well we might move on to *Helen*. As it turned out we were very happy with the work Dennis did for *Joy* and so we just kept going. Dennis's brief was very simple really but we talked a lot about certain sounds we wanted and the simplicity we were looking for, given the fact that we were also using voice-over in the film.

Despite the reaction to the perceived 'glacial' tone of the film, we see *Helen* as a deeply emotional film, where the emotional world of the film is very much raging under the surface. What we find compelling about Annie Townsend's performance is that she manages to express that hidden turmoil in a very restrained and subtle way. We very much wanted the music to respond to that quality we believed the film possessed. We didn't want to force or drive an emotional response from the audience; instead we wanted the film to open up a space for the audience. What was probably very good for us in the end was to work the edit almost to the point of picture lock without ever introducing the element of music.

We briefed Dennis by giving him a draft edit of the film, by talking to him, by sending responses back and forth and, ultimately, by trusting him to get on with it. The completed mix of the score didn't arrive in the UK until the week of the final Dolby mix of our film. Our feeling was, if the music doesn't work in the end we wouldn't include it. We had such a strong sense of the film and how it worked without the music that we trusted that *Helen* could work with it. However, as we lay the tracks on the timeline, we just knew that the music that Dennis had produced would work. In that way our collaboration with Dennis was very much in keeping with the spirit of the *Civic Life* series. It is a cinema of 'making do' whereby, despite the lead in the saddle at the beginning of the race, we trust that the groundwork and preparation we do ensures that something worthwhile and distinctive, if flawed, will make it through to the finishing post.

JW: *How, if at all, has the reaction to the film affected you?*

CM/JL: Don't forget that the origins of this film were to make a community project. None of the money (miniscule though it is in feature-film terms) came from film financing routes. So there was absolutely no commercial pressure on us, or the project. The aim was to make a film with local participation that fed back positively to the communities that were involved. Now this other level of the film festival circuit and nominations and latterly distribution has been something of a surprise to us also. That said, we had done enough short films to guess that if things worked out we could make something highly distinctive and interesting for this moment in time. When we use the term distinctive we are referring to a kind of film one doesn't normally see coming out of the UK or Ireland today. To our mind *Helen* is the kind of film that could have been at home in the 1950s in France. It could be argued that the unusual route through which it was funded led to an equally unusual film. At no stage did we have to sell the idea or package it to make it fundable by film financiers. We have a sense we will never get that opportunity ever again.

Helen has already been screened in many, many places. How it has affected us is not entirely clear just yet but it's certainly having a very positive affect on the journey towards getting our next feature film made. We say 'journey' as there is a long way to go yet but the basic idea and the writing are going well, and perhaps we sense that if we aim to have a chance at making a third feature film we need to refine some elements in our thinking and methodology.

JW: *I generally try to avoid asking about influences but Antonioni's name has appeared once or twice in connection to* **Helen**. *Are there any figures whose work has made a particular impression upon you?*

CM/JL: Yes, we are big fans of Antonioni. We would also add Atom Egoyan, Barbara Loden, Carl Theodor Dreyer, Miklós Jancsó and many others. We're happy about that. We can't say how accurate it is but it's clearly not off the mark and these are all filmmakers whose work we are very familiar with. If you play certain music to a baby whilst it's still in the womb, or as an infant, it affects the child in positive ways. Lots of osmosis. We love work that makes us think and challenges us and we could just as easily be referring to photography, or literature or writing. After all, isn't that one of the things about work that we love, how it influences our way of thinking?

Ray **Lawrence**

Lawrence's unique cinematic style has established him as one of the most respected dramatic directors of contemporary Australian cinema. While only producing three films in his 25-year career as a director, all of his features offer an intelligent and intense mediation around the slippery and often painful nature of human interaction and familial strife.

Lawrence's first feature was *Bliss* (1985), an adaptation of the Peter Carey novel. Co-scripted by the author himself, the film revolves around a successful advertising executive whose life is brought into sharp focus after surviving a near-death experience.

After a lengthy hiatus from features during which he became a much-in-demand commercials director, Lawrence returned in 2001 with *Lantana*. Examining the notion of trust, the film weaves the mysterious disappearance of a wealthy psychiatrist across the fabric of three Australian families, with each family representative of a different social class existent of contemporary Australian society. A critical and commercial success domestically and internationally, the film was awarded the Best Film prize at the Australian Film Institute Awards.

One of the most engrossing, thoughtful, adult-oriented dramas in many years, *Jindabyne* (2006) is a subtle, powerful, haunting film of visual beauty, mystery and moral horror; and not easily forgotten. On an annual fishing expedition in isolated high country, a group of men discover a girl's body in the water. Deciding to delay reporting their find once the trip is concluded, the decision precipitates tensions within the town and the wider Aboriginal community. The fallout is personal as well as political, with the marriage between Claire (Laura Linney), a withdrawn American, and Stewart (Gabriel Byrne), an Irish mechanic, particularly suffering as Claire embarks on a personal crusade in search of forgiveness.

Fashioning a compelling and complex drama of doubt, anger, shame and moral responsibility, Lawrence and screenwriter Beatrix Christian's transposition of Raymond Carver's short story *So Much Water, So Close To Home* to an Australian setting also makes for an incisive narrative about contemporary Australia and its sexual and racial climate.

JASON WOOD: *I saw* Jindabyne *in Cannes last year when you introduced the film to its first public audience.*

RAY LAWRENCE: I was pleased with the reaction; they can be hard to please. I like the idea of mystery in a film and I think that mystery in cinema is slowly being eroded. It's so rare that you discover a film. The last time I discovered a film I think was way back in the 1970s. It felt refreshing then to see a film and not know beforehand exactly what it was about and to be constantly told how fabulous it was. We managed to do this with *Lantana* to an extent because nobody really knew anything about that or if they did they weren't particularly interested. The fact that it was successful in some ways made *Jindabyne* harder for me because I also had to deal with expectation. I very much like the idea of going into a film without knowing too much about it. I even like the idea of then coming out of it and not being too sure, of having to think about it, to ponder what the spectator has just seen.

JW: *Despite attracting actors of the calibre of Laura Linney and Gabriel Byrne, and despite the success of* Lantana, *I've read that that* Jindaybyne *was hard to finance.*

RL: It was very hard and even having these actors on board wasn't really advantageous. I feel especially sorry for scriptwriters. They have to write for people who, in the main, don't understand the process and also don't trust the process. I've worked with a novelist [Peter Carey] and two playwrights [Andrew Bovell and Beatrix Christian] and they both write for the actors so what's really happening is between the lines. Those scripts, when you read them, don't provide any suggestion of a blockbuster or crossover film. I honestly don't understand the elements of success that constitute the ingredients of a successful script. Sure there are factors such as the trackrecord of the writer, the director, the actors etc, but it's constantly proven that this formula doesn't work. In fact no formula works; it's really just a horse race. The sort of films that interest me, I'm frankly amazed that I even get them made. I slip under the wire. I can certainly attract good writers and that's terrific, but I find it very difficult to then try to balance the commercial dictates of a film. For example, the process of cutting a trailer is very difficult. You want to stimulate people just enough so that they say, yes, I want to know more, but most companies want you to produce a trailer that explains absolutely everything. When you try to raise money in America it's the marketing department that calls the shots. It's a very cynical exercise. Art films are always looked at in terms of their potential crossover, which is a tremendous amount of pressure.

JW: *And are you able to disassociate yourself from these pressures?*

RL: I honestly just try to make the films that I would like to see. I totally trust and respect the audience and I don't want to let them down by suddenly trying to please them too much. I admire a lot of films produced in the 1970s, Coppola's *The Conversation* [1974] for instance, and these could be described as quite slow in the way that they unravel and reveal their secrets. This is a path that I've also tried to follow. I lament what television has done to us as audiences. There is a trend now to speed things up to the extent that what we watch is just colour and movement. As a result, as soon as you leave your seat you have forgotten what you have just seen.

JW: *To go back to Raymond Carver and his short story* So Much Water, So Close To Home, *what was it that attracted you to the material? I understand that you originally became interested in the story whilst making* Bliss.

RL: I think it was mainly the notion of responsibility. I've always been interested in this concept and the story clearly had that. It was only a very small story but it had some very big themes and that enabled me to hang a lot of other things on it that I found interesting. I also wanted to make it an Australian story about Australian characters.

JW: *The film has a lot to say about the racial and sexual climate in Australia.*

RL: The interest in these issues and in Australia in general is a pretty essential element of my work. We are a very multicultural country and it was important to me that the character of Stewart was Irish. I wanted a parallel with the Aboriginal experience, not only in terms of being oppressed, but in terms of the Irish being early inhabitants of the country. I feel very fortunate that I was able to make *Jindabyne* and retain these interesting themes in a filmmaking environment that is quite hostile to subtlety.

JW: *Your characters are often confronted by moral dilemmas. Do you see this as a foundation of your work?*

RL: It's the root of all drama. A good moral dilemma is something that anybody can identify with and understand. There are so many different opinions of a work that people can have and as a novelist or a filmmaker one of the greatest compliments is to have people discuss and ruminate over what you have done. Confronting your characters with these moral complexities is a wonderful way of provoking discussion. I've had discussions with people who have seen *Jindabyne* and they've seen things in it that I never even knew were there. This perhaps makes the film that much more dense.

I deliberately wanted to push the structure and the storytelling in *Jindabyne* so that there were deliberate pauses and, as a result, room for interpretation. I was influenced by David Lynch's *Lost Highway* [1997] in this regard. The structures of the film are obviously very different but I wanted there to be grey areas that people could interpret as they wished. For example, some people who see the film are annoyed by Claire's character because she is on everybody's case all the time. At moments she can be annoying, and we've all had friends that have taken on a particular cause and turned it into a crusade. I also want people to recognise things in their own lives in the stories that I am trying to tell. To me that is fantastic because then they are connected to it. Also, if they can't recognise your characters and the people in the film then they are never going to believe in the on-screen world that you have created. I'm also a huge fan of the work of Ken Loach and always find I'm able to relate to his films, no matter where they are set. I also like the fact that they are often about the concept of the family and of course about relationships. That Loach's films have such a strong political bent also really impresses me.

JW: *The character of Gregory takes the film into a whole new territory.*

RL: Gregory is an analogy for evil. Evil always has been with us and always will be with us. It's just never going to go away. You could step into a lift with a bunch of people and have no idea if one of the people in the crowd wishes to do you harm. I was also interested in the notion that people who are bad will be caught in the end and brought to justice; they clearly aren't always. It's quite terrifying that Gregory gets away with it and I think that this is realistic.

JW: *What part did the film's setting play?*

RL: I like fly-fishing and the area where the film is set – though a lot of the rivers have now dried up – is one of the parts in Australia where you can still do it. It's also a fairly mountainous area and in Aboriginal culture the highest point in the landscape is the most significant because they can see their country and their land. This makes the area where we shot very important to Aboriginal people.

The word 'jindabyne' actually means valley and the town was flooded and is now under water. This gives the notion of ghosts and the notion of things from your past returning to haunt you. Claire's ghost was her suffering from post-natal depression and, at least as far as Stewart is concerned, the resulting abandonment of her son.

Once Beatrix and I had secured the rights we went up to Jindabyne in New South Wales and just walked around like a couple of journalists looking at characters and potential locations. It was whilst doing this that we found stories and inspirations that were in the actual area and incorporated these into the Raymond Carver story. We very much wanted to make sure that the film felt very connected to the area.

JW: *Yourself and DP David Williamson like to work with natural light and with your landscape. What kind of elements did this enable you to tease out?*

RL: Well, when you work in the kind of landscape we did you'd be stupid to ignore it so we made a conscious decision to make it a character in the film. I think I'd also trace my fondness for working with available light back to my love of Ken Loach. It does affect the actors. The less paraphernalia in the eyeline of the actors, the more natural their performances I find. I also find it off-putting for them if they are trying to focus and all around them are huge numbers of crew members sitting around in baseball caps. It's all about trying to have less distractions.

The actors are the conduit for the story and the more relaxed and natural they are, the more they can take the audience out of simply being in the cinema. Cinema is quite a primal thing if you think about it, almost like a group of strangers sitting in a cave. You can still walk up to the projector and put your hand in front of it and the image is gone. Take your hand away and the image is there again. Technically, I find that you don't need superfluous elements when shooting. I guess that if we are making a very stylised film and want to create a different world then maybe, but I prefer to move away from what may be considered a throw back to the old days when you were expected to have all this equipment and all this lighting. Remember also that I always work on location and never on sets so I want to reflect the world that we are working in so that you can maybe recognise it. Even when we shot interiors, in kitchens etc, we preferred to use the lights that were already there. We simply turned them on. I'd like to hope that an audience subconsciously recognises that.

JW: *Gabriel Byrne commented that he was persuaded to make Jindabyne because you claimed that it would offer an important spiritual experience. Does this also play a part for you with regards to the projects you choose?*

RL: We are very fortunate to do what we do, and if we are working with like-minded people in a like-minded way and trying to reflect some semblance of life as it is lived then you are working towards a common goal. This undoubtedly has a spiritual quality to it. Now, with this particular project, if you marry all those elements to the mountain range in which we were working then I would hope that you would take something away from the experience. When I met Gabriel in New York I certainly told him that I hoped it would be a spiritually fulfilling experience. I'm pleased he responded to that.

JW: *Your films seem to connect both with audiences and critics and so I wondered, as someone who is obviously somewhat resistant to filmmaking by committee, if you would be resistant to overtures to work in America?*

RL: Gabriel told me that he worked on a Hollywood film directed by a European – and I'll be discreet – and they would start at 6am and by 10.30 in the evening they still hadn't shot anything because there was a group of executives sitting by the monitor and every time the director set up a shot they would offer suggestions on it. It would be impossible to work in those circumstances, for the crew and for the actors; there would be no vibrancy to it. I don't like doing a lot of takes for this very reason. The scene in the film where Gabriel and Laura have a fight, that's the only take that we did. It was just so powerful, frightening and kind of fittingly embarrassing that when they asked if I wanted them to do it again I couldn't think of what they could possibly do to add to it. I wouldn't be able to do this under a mainstream American feature. I'd be given the sack. I'd also be wary of everything being smoothed out and made easy on a big film. Just to get to the location the actors would often have to negotiate a long walk, perhaps a river crossing, and even snakes and to have all that made easy… I think that you would lose something. A certain energy is often taken away with money.

I'd certainly be interested in working outside Australia. However. I'm working on two projects right now. One deals with the aftermath of the Bosnian conflict. The other, a collaboration with Anthony LaPaglia, is an adaptation of Arthur Miller's *A View From the Bridge*. The screenplay for *A View From the Bridge* was written by Andrew Bovell with Miller's blessing and is fantastic. Anthony played the part of Eddie on Broadway and received a Tony award and I've spoken with Frances McDormand about playing Eddie's wife, Beatrice. I'd shoot the whole thing in black and white. This takes me back to where we began, I just can't raise the money, not even with all these constituent elements. I wouldn't change the way I'd work, and I think there'd still be an audience for it.

James **Marsh**

After graduating from Oxford University, James Marsh worked as a researcher and then a director for the BBC. Marsh's breakthrough documentary, *Troubleman* (1994), chronicled the last years of Marvin Gaye and his murder at the hands of his father. *The Burger and the King* (1996), a documentary about Elvis Presley's bizarre eating habits, and a documentary profile of John Cale (1998) swiftly followed.

Wider attention came with *Wisconsin Death Trip* (1999), a dramatized documentary about a small town in Wisconsin blighted by outbreaks of suicide, murder and insanity in the 1890s. Marsh won a BAFTA award for the film along with a Best Documentary prize from the Royal Television Society.

The King (2005) marked Marsh's move away from documentary into pure fiction. Like his contemporary Kevin Macdonald, Marsh would prove adept at moving seamlessly between the two mediums. An Official Selection at Cannes, the film is a slow-burning tale of jealousy and revenge set in a born-again Christian community in Texas. Gael Garcia Bernal and William Hurt excel in the central roles. Unfairly overlooked on release, the film has since grown in stature.

After photographing, directing and editing *The Team* (2005), a collaboration with Basia Winograd, which charts the efforts of a group of homeless men in New York City to organise a football team to compete in the inaugural Homeless World Cup in Graz, Austria, Marsh's career went stratospheric with *Man on Wire* (2008).

On 7 August 1974, a young Frenchman named Philippe Petit stepped out on a wire illegally rigged between the twin towers of New York's World Trade Center, then the world's tallest buildings. After nearly an hour dancing on the wire, he was arrested, taken for psychological evaluation and brought to jail before he was finally released. A skilful blend of archive footage and reconstruction, Marsh's powerful and entertaining documentary brings Petit's extraordinary adventure to life through the testimony of Philippe himself, and some of the co-conspirators who helped him create the unique and magnificent spectacle that became known as 'the artistic crime of the century'.

Since this interview took place Marsh has also completed *Project Nim* (2011), a provocative account of the extraordinary journey of Nim Chimpsky, a chimpanzee who in the 1970s became the focus of a radical experiment which aimed to prove that an ape could learn to communicate using sign language if raised and nurtured like a human child. There has also been a return to fiction with *Shadow Dancer* (2012). Adapted from the novel by Tom Bradby, the film concerns a young IRA member (played by Andrea Riseborough) who is forced to turn informant for MI5 in order to protect her young son.

———

JASON WOOD: *I understand that the film's producer, Simon Chinn, heard Philippe Petit speaking on* **Desert Island Discs** *and the film developed from that.*

JAMES MARSH: Indeed he did. And that really piqued his interest, both in Philippe, who has a powerful presence in every medium, and specifically his adventures at the World Trade Center. He then tracked Philippe down and began the process of optioning Philippe's book *To Reach the Clouds*. Meanwhile, I live in New York and like many people, I was dimly aware of Philippe's walk between the Twin Towers in the 1970s. It's a piece about the city's recent folklore. Simon called me to casually sound me out about the possibility of doing a film based on the story. It took me about two seconds to realise what a brilliant idea it was and as soon as I read the book, I knew I absolutely had to make the film. So the project started for me with Philippe's book.

JW: *Several other producers had attempted and failed to bring Philippe's tale to the screen. What was it about this project that gained his consent and collaboration?*

JM: Well, we persevered and wouldn't take no for an answer. Philippe brushed Simon off initially and when I approached him, we had a very awkward and prickly conversation on the phone. But this just made us want to do it even more. I then wrote him a long letter outlining my plans for the film and on the basis of that he granted me an audience in person. As soon as we met we got on. I said the magic words that no one had said before: 'It's your story. I want to collaborate with you on it.' It was on that basis that we preceded. It wasn't all plain sailing and there were passionate disagreements along the way. It was also a lot of fun. I've never enjoyed making a film as much as I did this one. I think also the timing was right. Everyone involved is now getting on a bit and of course, the destruction of the towers adds another dimension to Philippe's story, one that nobody could have foreseen.

JW: *Your material deals not only with a legendary quest and a pursuit of dreams but also has a love story element.*

JM: First off, I just loved the fairytale quality but the more I looked into the criminal aspects of the undertaking, the more I understood that the film could – and should – be a kind of heist movie. It was important to tell the story in a gripping and exciting way and so I pushed a whole range of documentary techniques as far as they could go to make the film a big-screen experience. But you're right, the story has many, many layers and most of them are just generated and exposed by telling the story itself. At various points in the film it is a love story, between Philippe and his long-suffering companion Annie, but there is a third party too, Philippe and his tightrope. It's also a story about friendship and its limits. The success of the venture couldn't salvage the relationships that had been strained to breaking point by the collective effort to do something that to all intents and purposes should have been impossible.

So there was a very different and perhaps more positive spectrum of emotions in this material than in anything I'd done before. My previous film, *The King*, was a tough film to write and make. Looking back on it, I think it's a pretty cruel and unforgiving piece of work. However, it wasn't the subject matter that got to me, it was the process of actually getting it funded and in production that disillusioned me about making low-budget features in the US. As a career move, it was also a disaster. The film didn't lose anyone any money, apart from the people who were creatively involved like my co-writer and producer, Milo Addica, producer Jim Wilson and of course me. In fact, it made people money. But perception is everything in the US. I made a nasty piece of work that was deemed financially unsuccessful and that was it. There was no way I could ever make another feature in the US. So there was consolation and relief to be found in working with established and trustworthy British producers – both Simon and Jonathan Hewes at Wall to Wall were brilliant throughout the production. The perfect producers, they took care of all the business, trusted me to make the film and had intelligent advice about how it was progressing. But you're right. It was personally liberating to delve into the heist genre, comedy, and the sheer thrill ride of Philippe's story.

JW: *How did you and Philippe set about working together to craft the shape that* Man on Wire *would take?*

JM: We sat around and drank a lot. I did most of the listening in our early meetings. I wanted to know everything that Philippe recalled about his adventure. Then I went away and wrote a detailed treatment and worked out the structure and flashbacks and overlapping timelines that you see in the finished film.

Philippe had wanted to make his own film and that did create friction at times.

He didn't always understand what I was doing or how a film is constructed and so he was often very critical when I showed him rushes. Other times we fought about who should be in the film and we had a pretty major tussle over the ending. At certain points I felt I was protecting his story from the ideas he had about telling it. However, we also had enormous fun. We never fell out personally and we've remained friends. Our fights were always about the work. It was good to be challenged and criticised as I made the film, it made me examine my choices carefully. And it made the film better.

JW: *Did you study other heist films?*

JM: After I finished the film, I realised that it had pretty much the same structure as *Reservoir Dogs* [1992], which also has an unfolding present-tense crime narrative and a series of extended flashbacks that contextualise the ongoing narrative. But I knew my structure going in and had played around with unusual structures before in documentaries. After shooting, I usually do the first cut of a film on my own without an editor and that's where I work out the structure. That way, you become really familiar with the material and you can mess around and try things out without any pressure. I have a very close relationship with my editor, Jinx Godfrey, and she's not at all precious about me cutting on my own at certain points in the edit. That said, her contribution to all my films has been immense; it's been my one constant collaboration and I can't imagine making a film without her. Our relationship in the cutting room is almost telepathic.

Before the making of the film, I recalled *Rififi* [1955] in my head, Jules Dassin's beautifully made French heist film but I didn't actually watch it. I looked at Fritz Lang's *M* [1931] with my DP Igor Martinovic. It is actually about a child killer in the Weimar Republic but it has lots of chases and hiding out and is beautifully and expressively shot. We also looked at how the reconstructions worked in Errol Morris's *The Thin Blue Line* [1998] and Murnau's *Nosferatu* [1922] for its use of shadow and silhouette. For pleasure and inspiration, I watched *La Strada* [1954] and the very odd and charming documentaries of Patrick Keillor and Andrew Kötting.

JW: *As well as the astonishing footage, the richness of the story also comes from the power of Philippe's recollection and a preference for acting out events. Is this purely a reflection of his personality or do you feel he was also inspired by the powerful memories and emotions?*

JM: He wanted to tell the story unencumbered by the usual trappings of a formal interview. In fact, we started shooting a conventional interview with him but it quickly descended into chaos as he started leaping about and hopping around the room. After a brief moment of panic, the DP and I embraced the situation for what it was. If Philippe wants to tell his story with all this energy and passion and he wants to run around the room and act bits out for us, then we need to facilitate that. So we did and it was very liberating for all of us and we began to make our own contributions. The DP got up on a ladder for some of the 'interview' and shot most of it hand-held, chasing Philippe around the room. At one point, he disappeared behind a curtain. So this brought a real energy to both his recollections and the film. It's definitely a performance but it is coming from a complete physical as well as mental immersion in the events he was recalling. It's like the best kind of acting where he was fully connecting to real, experienced emotion. Obviously, Philippe has told this story many times but rarely in such detail and just occasionally I would provoke him by interrupting him or by theatrically whispering to the DP if I felt he was just rehearsing an anecdote.

JW: *Was it always the intention to have the participation of figures such as Jean-Louis Blondeau, Jim Moore etc, and given the history of both loyalty and tension what different perspectives to the story did you hope their testimonies would bring?*

JM: It was. Philippe's book is in the first person but it mentions all these interesting characters who helped and sometimes hindered him along the way. It was vital to the film's narrative to include detailed testimony from everyone who was involved in the planning and execution of the crime. It allowed the film to have multiple overlapping narratives and points of view and dramatic conflict. As in any collective human endeavour, there was a great deal of tension and antagonism and opening up the film to other voices makes it a real human drama. Interestingly, almost everyone concurred on the most preposterous and unbelievable aspects of the story; the conflict was in how they felt about each other.

Fortunately, I managed to track everyone down. There was the French contingent whom Philippe had known and trusted for years, his girlfriend Annie, his closest friend at the time Jean Louis and his delightful friend, Jean François. These were the true believers. Jean Louis played a crucial role in the planning of the break in and in a real sense took responsibility for his friend's life. He rigged the wire on the North Tower which Philippe couldn't check for obvious reasons so he just had to trust that Jean Louis had done it right. Given all the problems they had up there, that was no small thing. Jean Louis also provided a detailed account of the events in the North Tower, including a lot of new details that even Philippe didn't know. Jean Louis is also a very different kind of personality to Philippe. He's grounded and practical and not given to taking risks, believe it or not. They squabbled fiercely throughout the planning stage and they're still squabbling about it in the film. Sadly, their friendship didn't survive the achievement.

In the film, Jean Louis, the least emotional man in the whole adventure, becomes the most emotional interviewee. He is pained enormously by the fracturing of his friendship with Philippe and it is very moving to see a man like that so bitterly regret how things turned out. Annie provided a crucial emotional perspective for the film. She was very much in love with Philippe and early on in the film she describes how he seduced her. She endured a lot for her passion, not least supporting Philippe on ventures where she felt he was risking his life. After he had performed his walk and was released from jail, he has a lusty tumble with a female admirer, which also must have been painful for her. Some reviewers of the film have castigated Philippe for his infidelity but who wouldn't have been tempted by the prospect of a quickie with a beautiful stranger? I know I would… Meanwhile, Annie describes their separation after the walk in very forgiving terms and that's how the film presents it.

Along the way, Philippe picked up a number of more or less reliable allies. Mark Lewis, the Australian, came up with some important practical suggestions – though he didn't see it through. They made an aborted attempt to break in to the towers but Mark didn't think they were ready and backed off. He was probably right. He's a lovely man and a very good filmmaker in his own right – he made the brilliant *Cane Toads* [1988]. Jim Moore was another helper who also got very nervous about the risks and refused to go into the towers and help with the rigging though he stuck around and helped in various ways. Along with his trusted French allies, Philippe ended up going into the towers with two rather feckless Americans who he had met very casually. They were pretty hard to track down but well worth it. David (who Philippe insists on calling Donald) was a singer-songwriter at the time (and a talented one) but he smoked a lot of pot and he went in stoned. He ended up running out of the towers when they had to hide out from a guard and that was that. He was another delightful character whom I liked a lot – he's completely honest and very funny about his personal shortcomings. The final assistant was Alan (Albert as far as Philippe is concerned). Philippe was adamantly opposed to including 'Albert' in the film and we fought a lot about that. Alan himself was also very reluctant to be in the film but I wouldn't take no for an answer. Finally, he gave in, at the last minute, just as I was about to go to London to fine cut. His testimony was invaluable. He went into the North Tower with Jean Louis and they didn't like each other from the get go. They both wanted to be in charge but they couldn't actually understand each other – neither spoke the other's language so it became a kind of French farce. After they lost the wire in the void, Alan basically gives up because he thinks it's impossible to pull the wire in before dawn. He was wrong about that; Jean Louis did pull it in and it was the final miracle that preceded the walk itself. Again, Alan doesn't come out of it very well but I don't think they would have pulled it off without him.

Because we don't have any moving footage of the walk itself, allowing all these people to describe and re-connect with their experience of seeing the walk itself becomes the emotional high point of the film. They all still marvel at what they achieved and remember it in vivid, compelling detail and each one at some point becomes overwhelmed by the emotions they recall.

JW: *Another interesting facet of* Man on Wire *is the depiction of a bygone New York and America in general.*

JM: Well, the story very specifically happens in New York at the World Trade Center in August 1974. In fact, it could only have happened then for many reasons, not least Philippe's narrow window of opportunity to conquer them was when they had been physically completed but not fully occupied and with some remaining work to be done on the roofs. If he had delayed by even a week, he couldn't have rigged his wire – the ribbon of metal sheeting at the very top was being put in place and it was half way round when he did the walk (you can see it in the photos) so he was still able to use the exposed pipes at the top to lash the wire. The whole Watergate scandal came to a head that week and Nixon resigned just after the walk so Philippe shares the headlines with that major political event.

The fate of the Twin Towers is this unmanageable subtext in the film but I felt that if I confined the story to the specifics of Philippe's adventure and saw the buildings through his obsessive perspective, I could take some of the curse off the buildings, at least for the duration of the film. He dreamed about doing the walk before the buildings were even built so that allowed us to see the ongoing construction of them from the foundations up. It's actually a discreet timeline in the film; their slow grand march up to the sky over years as Philippe keeps his eye on them and performs other illegal walks around the world.

In many ways, the film is nostalgic but I hope not sentimental. Nostalgia has a troubling ache to it – the pain of time that you can remember, almost touch but not fully recover. *Man on Wire* evokes a world that we have allowed ourselves to lose, particularly in New York City. It's hardly an innocent time but it seems more tolerant and forgiving. You can't imagine Guiliani allowing Philippe to get away with what he did with no real punishment. You can't imagine a group of foreigners breezing into the airport with a bow and arrow in their suitcase or hanging around a major New York monument taking photos and notes. So the film reclaims that time and by remembering Philippe's walk in such detail I hope there is a victory of memory over time and a reminder of what we have become and what we have lost.

JW: *It must have been a conscious decision to make no mention of the events of 11 September 2001.*

JM: It was the very first decision I made and it was emphatically underscored in every pitch and proposal I made when we trying to get funding for the film. Of course there are interesting (perhaps disturbing) analogies in Philippe's plot to conquer the towers and some of the imagery in the film is very suggestive to us now. The whole illegal plot by foreigners, people looking up at the towers in awe (not horror), a plane flying over Philippe as he walked. But all those connections were created by future events and exist in our minds – they are not implicit in what Philippe and his friends did in 1974. It's not prophetic – it's just a brilliant adventure undertaken by young people who refuse to accept that such a thing is impossible.

And quite simply nothing we could say or show or discuss in our film would be worthwhile in the face of the later tragedy. It would be cheap and wrong. I very much disliked that shot in the Spielberg film *Munich* [2005] where there is a slow and pointed pan to the Twin Towers. I suppose it's intended to be profound in some way but it seemed heavy handed and trite.

I was acutely aware of the fact that everyone watching the film was going to have a response predicated on knowledge of the towers' destruction. That was actually reassuring – as long as I told the story well, I could let the audience complete the film for themselves on that level. I have my own very strong feelings on that score. I lived in New York for 14 years and I watched those buildings come down with my own eyes, so did hundreds of thousands of other New Yorkers, if not millions. I shot news footage for the BBC in the city that day and actually filmed Building 7 come down in the evening. I had a friend who died in the buildings. That's not something I ever talked about when the film was released but it remains a very painful fact. So, this was a very personal film for me to make and the last thing I wanted to do was trade in that obscene imagery. I wanted to make something beautiful – or rather celebrate something that I found very beautiful and in so many ways, the inverse of what happened thirty years later.

JW: *As well as the film's distinct visual sensibility is the adroit use of Michael Nyman music. How do you feel the score complements both the film's visual and it's thematic concerns?*

JM: When we were preparing the film, I used to go up to Philippe's house in upstate New York and watch him practice on the wire. He likes to rehearse to music and amongst an eclectic soundtrack of gypsy music and classical pieces there was Michael Nyman's *Memorial* from the Peter Greenaway's *The Cook, The Thief, His Wife and Her Lover* [1989]. I couldn't place it at first but it was so appropriate to the pomp and majesty of Philippe's unusual style of tight-rope walking. So that's where the idea came from initially.

Of course, we couldn't afford to commission an original score from Michael but he did agree to meet me. Based on my enthusiasm for *Memorial*, it was actually his idea to create a soundtrack from his back catalogue. He just opened up every thing for us, all the music he controlled and owned the publishing on. It was literally like a kid being let loose in a sweet shop. I spent two weeks in

London spotting in the music on my own and it seemed to work, even though we were using some pieces that would be familiar to some filmgoers. Michael's music makes the film BIG. There's nothing tentative about it. Its loud, monumental, all consuming, exactly like Philippe's performances. I always felt that Michael's music dominates the films he scores, sometimes it overwhelms them. But in *Man on Wire* we had a protagonist and a performance that could absorb the music, and that was equal to its grandeur. For the record, I also used a discreet original score for all the heist scenes in the film – the black and white reconstructions. As I was about to lock the film, I panicked. We were using the *Memorial* theme for all those scenes and its power was being diminished by repetition. So I asked a friend of mine, Josh Ralph, to have a look at those scenes and he came up with a gripping and playful set of themes that carry those scenes more discreetly. We didn't have any money to pay him at that point and so he very kindly just gave them to the film. We only use *Memorial* for the walk itself and it grabs you and shakes you up, I think.

JW: *The act has been described as the 'artistic crime of the century' and Philippe's distrust of authority from an early age is very clear. Do you feel that this is another of the reasons why people so immediately identify with him and with the film in general?*

JM: Well, that's why I immediately identified with Philippe and what he does. It's truly subversive without being destructive. I'm sure some people might resist it on that level – what Philippe does is completely pointless – it has no objective beyond itself. But look at the objective: he creates ephemeral moments of beauty that not only defy human authority but challenge the laws of nature, almost. I never questioned the value or the point of what Philippe does and neither does the film. I am just thrilled and exhilarated that he has done these amazing walks that have miraculously unfolded like a dream for passers-by, the lucky, uninvited audience. Any worthwhile artistic endeavour should by definition and necessity be an act of rebellion and revelation. In Philippe's case, it's also framed by the real possibility of death.

Philippe never talks about the risks of what he does but at one point in the film, he lets slip a very interesting phrase when he confronts the mind-boggling prospect of walking on a tightrope at the top of the Twin Towers: 'to die in the exercise of your passion … what a beautiful death'. You can take it or leave it but there's no question that he means it and indeed lives his life that way. What he does is at the limit of human possibility. He's not Batman or Superman; he's real flesh and blood. Perhaps that's the ultimate appeal of the film. It's a real-life fairytale.

Christopher **Nolan**

I know what you're thinking. The introduction and all those words about marginalised directors being given a voice and yet here's an interview with the director of the rejuvenated Batman franchise. Well, this happens to be an interview from very early on in Nolan's career when he was on the cusp of breaking through. Nolan doesn't actually happen to give that many interviews and I think this piece is instructive in terms of it being a glimpse into the methodology of a director who brings intellect and inventiveness to big-budget projects. It also shows how his interest in the cerebral and his favouring of non-linear narratives, elements that are very much present in his multi-million-dollar-budget outings.

Having experimented with Super-8mm at an early age, Nolan made his feature debut with *Following* (1988). A low-budget noir thriller co-written with his brother Jonathan, the film gained credibility on the festival circuit and led to increased financing for *Memento* (2000), the film with which Nolan made his name and the feature that precipitated this interview. A breakthrough film also for Guy Pearce, this riveting thriller about short-term memory loss is an enigma wrapped inside a puzzle. A highly regarded remake of the Swedish thriller *Insomnia* (2002), a film that proved that Nolan was very comfortable working on big budgets with stars to spare. Al Pacino, Hilary Swank and a surprisingly good Robin Williams all feature.

The opportunity to direct *Batman Begins* (2005) sent Nolan's career stratospheric and heralded a new era of intelligently-scripted superhero movies that placed characterisation on an even level with CGI and fight sequences. *The Dark Knight* (2008) and *The Dark Knight Rises* (2012) concluded the billion-dollars-plus-grossing trilogy. *The Prestige* (2006) reunited Nolan with Christian Bale for a whip-smart look at the dark art of magic and obsessive rivalry. Nolan's other film as a director – his most recent credit as a producer is Zack Snyder's *Man of*

Steel (2013), a rather lightweight Dark Knight facsimile – is the mind-bending sci-fi thriller Inception (2010), one of the most critically revered blockbusters in recent memory.

―――――

JASON WOOD: *Following the much praised* Following *you have moved on to a much bigger canvas with* Memento. *Was this always your intention?*

CHRISTOPHER NOLAN: It is what I've always wanted but it is also really daunting to go from having total control and doing your own little thing with your friends to having a financial responsibility with people watching and so on. But to be honest the process was similar and I enjoyed it. It was all the things I thought I was good at doing, namely visualising the film as it goes on, only on a bigger scale.

JW: *Despite the presence of Guy Pearce and Carrie Ann Moss the film still feels very intimate. Was this a mood and creative process that you were keen to retain from* Following?

CN: Definitely. It seemed like a claustrophobic story, even from when my younger brother first described it to me. It was intimate from the point of fact that the story is told from the point of view of a character that sits in a room and he has no idea what's outside the door. We shot the film in scope with anamorphic lenses because I wanted as clear an image as possible to really put the audience in the lead character's head. Once you start playing with the landscape you begin to feel a lot of texture and a lot of intimacy. Also, the way the film was shot contributes to this; there are very few wide shots, very few long shots and no establishing shots at all.

JW: *You take a lot of risks with the narrative.*

CN: I grew up with narrative experimentalism in many mediums, especially novels and in literature. Filmmakers should be able to experiment with narrative without alienating the audience and without creating something that's impenetrable, something that is highly textured. I was looking particularly at what Nicolas Roeg was doing in the 1970s and with his work there is a kind of abstraction that for wider audiences could have been unsatisfying. I actually see myself as a very mainstream filmmaker, albeit one that uses some of those narrative freedoms that Roeg and his kind were pushing for but applying them to a more concrete narrative. Even though audiences aren't going to get the answers to all of the questions in the film and it is a kind of unsettling in lots of ways, you'll find if you care to watch *Memento* a couple of times; it's pretty much all in there. One of the things I've been most satisfied about by the film is that it really lives on in people's heads.

JW: *One of the secrets of the film is the editing. Tell us about Dody Dorn's work.*

CN: Dody was a sound engineer for years, working largely with James Cameron, and the editing work she had done previously to *Memento* was very different. What I was looking for in an editor was someone who would give a different take on an emotional level and Dody really put that into the film. Within scenes she put up all kinds of little touches that make a big difference to getting across to the audience the notion that you cannot trust everything that you see.

JW: *One of the most striking themes of the film is the utter inconsequence of actions and indeed emotions such as revenge and jealousy.*

CN: All that was initially in Jonathan's story. For me it was such a wedge to open up these questions. Revenge is a particularly interesting concept, especially the notion of whether or not it exists outside of just an abstract idea, especially to somebody like Leonard who simply cannot perceive it. What has been interesting about the film is the differing reactions to it from young and old audiences. Elder viewers are less comfortable with it because the film pretty much comes down on the side of the idea that a lot of these things are meaningless and that we are living within our own heads. As people get older this notion becomes more frightening.

JW: *Did you always have your lead actors in mind?*

CN: I try not to have actors in mind when I write because the tendency then is to just write one of their characters that you have seen, either their last performance or your favourite of their performances. I try and write more abstractions, created characters and fictional characters and then you get to that very exciting point where you think, right, now who can play this role? In the case of Leonard it could have been played by all manner of different ages of actors. What I was really looking for was somebody extremely talented who could really carry this movie because Leonard is not only in almost very scene he is also in almost every shot. When I met Guy Pearce it was very clear that he had an enthusiasm for the project and was extremely meticulous and committed, which he had to be because we shot in 25 days so it was an extraordinary schedule.

JW: *It was good to see Joe Pantoliano in a bigger role.*

CN: Joe, who I primarily remember from *Risky Business* [1983], was introduced to me by Carrie Ann Moss and I immediately wanted to work with him because he was such a fun guy. He also bought a tremendous amount to the film in that he was the one person Leonard thought he had completely down and yet it was Joe's character who proved to have all the answers and who undermined Leonard's exposition.

JW: *The whole Sammy Jankis element of the story was extremely sensitively handled. How much research did you do into the very real condition of short-term memory loss?*

CN: My brother was taking a psychology class, which was how the idea came to him, so he had some understanding of the subject. I also did a little bit of research but I didn't want to do too much because I wanted to avoid getting bogged down in the realism of the condition, I was more interested in the metaphorical potential. Lots of people relate Leonard's condition to the experience to Alzheimer's, which perhaps goes back to why older people find the film more difficult to watch.

JW: *Is Jonathan happy with the finished product?*

CN: He's into it and is pretty proud of what we managed to put together.

Christian **Petzold**

Christian Petzold is widely regarded as one of the leading directors of contemporary German cinema. Making his feature debut with the political drama *The State I Am In* (2000), Petzold's other works include *Wolfsburg* (2003) and *Ghosts* (2005).

Petzold's films are marked by their interest in psychology and characters whose lives have been somehow torn loose from their moorings. One of his frequent collaborations with actor Nina Hoss, *Yella* (2007) brought the director's work to wider international attention. The story of a woman attempting to escape a volatile relationship by taking a job with a financial corporation in a new town, the film utilised striking sound design to evoke a hypnotic dreamlike quality.

The interview below took place around the release of *Barbara* (2012). Petzold's best-received work to date, the film is an impressively low-key account of a female doctor whose application for an exit visa from the GDR sees her transferred to a small rural community as punishment. Exploring personal and professional relations and the chasm between what we desire and a more humdrum reality, Petzold is once again well served by Hoss and his key creative nucleus of production designer Kade Gruber and director of photography Hans Fromm.

JASON WOOD: *During your research for* Barbara *did you speak with lots of people who had had an experience similar to that of your central character?*

CHRISTIAN PETZOLD: My parents were from East Germany and were refugees at the beginning of the 1960s. Their story of the communist system in the 1950s was

Yella, Christian Petzold, 2007 (Artificial Eye)

never a subject in our family, so I didn't know that as I was growing up. Then after 1989 they started to reflect on that time, the time of a communist regime. They had dreams that it would be an anti-fascist state from 1949 but instead it was a stony-cold government.

After reading the novels of Herman Broch I became more interested. He was writing at the beginning of the 1930s and the novel upon which my film is based dealt with a communist state in which a female doctor lived and was politically active underground whilst working in a children's hospital. This little novel was one of my favourites in the 1980s when I studied literature. When I started research, it became the basis of my work for *Barbara*.

Then I talked to doctors from the German Democratic Republic. At this time if you were politically outspoken you could go to jail for three or four months but because they needed doctors in the GDR they were sentenced to a solitary month. After release, however, they were sent to hospitals in the provinces as a sanction. During our rehearsals we talked about this as many actors grew up in the German Democratic Republic. One person we spoke to was a member of the Berliner Ensemble, the group that performed Brecht's plays in the West. Performing for this company offered the chance of escape. Nina Hoss spoke to one of these performers who explained with detail and sensitivity the subterfuge that she had to carry out in order to mask plans for defection.

JW: *One of your central concepts is absence. Many of the characters, Barbara especially, feel as if they are barely present in their own lives. Barbara in fact feels like a ghost.*

CP: This ghost idea is something I am very interested in. It was central to *Yella*. When you want to defect, on the last day you are like a ghost in that you are removed from society. Ghosts are always very lonely. Barbara is a ghost in between the West and East, today and tomorrow, and therefore she doesn't want to be sentimental, she does not want to show feelings. She doesn't know the place she is sent to. She is on the borderline and in transit.

JW: *What was your approach to the theme of love? The bond that develops between Barbara and Andre is very tentatively teased out and you avoid a fairytale depiction of the power of love. People fall in love but the harsh realities of life are frequent barriers…*

CP: It is a worldwide problem that people think that love will heal all and that love is the answer. For the German Democratic Republic the police had no problem extracting information from couples.

JW: *What were some of the film texts that you looked at in preparation?*

CP: Fassbinder was important. He portrays the ghosts of Western Germany and examines the melodramatic structures of German social life. I like the way that Howard Hawks uses dialogue. The most important is Roberto Rossellini and particularly *Stromboli* [1950]. Ingrid Bergman becomes like a ghost in the film and for me it is the best film about ghosts.

JW: *Where did you shoot? Were you able to use locations or did you have to work on studio sets?*

CP: After the 1945 bombings they rebuilt West Germany and it is difficult to find older buildings. But in the German Democratic Republic they couldn't afford to rebuild all the architecture so you find modern and period property existing alongside each other. You have the industrial buildings of the 1920s and Neo-Capitalist structures beside each other. You can find parts of cities of the Baltic Sea that look exactly like the 1920s and 1940s. The only things you have to remove are the satellite dishes. People got angry with us about that, as it meant temporarily loosing their Internet and TV. We undertook a voyage through these areas with the actors, having them take in the architecture as part of the rehearsal process. We found an empty hospital and renovated it from photographs of the period. It was so authentic that people that visited it that had worked in such hospitals described it as being similar to going back in time.

JW: *I understand that you shot chronologically.*

CP: This is a challenging and expensive process but for *Barbara* I thought it was essential, especially in terms of the relationship between Barbara and Andre. In many ways the film is a documentary of this developing relationship development. The only sequence shot out of sequence was the kiss. It didn't feel right saving such a grand gesture for the end of the film so we simply shot it when the moment felt right.

Nicolas **Winding Refn**

Nicolas Winding Refn was born in Copenhagen, relocating a number of times throughout his youth to New York. Expelled from the American Academy of Dramatic Arts, Refn's acceptance into the Danish Film School was also curtailed when he dropped out prior to the start of term.

Writing, directing and starring in a short made for an obscure Danish TV channel, Refn was given the opportunity of a lifetime when the short was seen by a group of producers who offered him 3.2 million kroner to turn it into a feature. That became the stylish, violent and uncompromising *Pusher* (1996), which established Refn's acute visual style and refusal to shy away from the graphic depiction of violence. The film quickly became a cult phenomenon, spawning the sequels *Bleeder* (1999), *With Blood On My Hands: Pusher II* (2004) and *I'm the Angel of Death: Pusher III* (2005).

Refn's first foray into English-language work was the US-set *Fear X*. Co-written with Hubert Selby Jr and starring John Turturro, the film premiered at Sundance in 2003. A somewhat uneven work, it is eclipsed by Refn's second English-language feature, the ultra-stylised *Bronson* (2009). Featuring a career-making performance by Tom Hardy as the eponymous Bronson, Britain's most notorious career criminal, the film's use of Scott Walker's 'The Electrician' also marked out Refn's singular approach to music.

The near-silent *Valhalla Rising* (2009) reunited Refn and Mads Mikkelsen. A mythical tale of a one-eyed warrior, the film has clear parallels with Herzog's *Aguirre, Wrath of God* (1972) and made tremendous use of its remote Scottish landscapes.

This interview took place around the release of *Drive* (2011). An adaptation of the novel by James Sallis, this violent crime film took Refn's career to new heights, achieving both critical and commercial success and establishing a somewhat unlikely ongoing collaboration with taciturn leading man Ryan Gosling. The pair have since completed the divisive *Only God Forgives* (2013), an existential revenge drama set amidst the seedy underage sex joints and boxing clubs of Bangkok.

JASON WOOD: *How did you come to the novel by James Sallis and what was it about the book that attracted you in terms of adapting it?*

NICOLAS WINDING REFN: The novel is more narrative-driven but what really interested me was making the driver into a superhero-type figure. In many ways he is a classic superhero and because of this he is very much forced to exist on the margins. He's denied romantic involvement with Irene – though he can't help falling in love with her – almost by his very nature, and yet as a result of his nature he is compelled to adopt the role of her protector and actually sacrifice his own happiness on her behalf.

JW: *You filmed on location in Los Angeles and yet in the tradition of John Boorman's* Point Blank *[1967] bring an outsider's eye to the city.*

NWR: There are actually a number of parallels between *Drive* and *Point Blank*. *Point Blank* was made because Lee Marvin admired John Boorman and wanted to make a movie with him and so kind of petitioned to bring him out to L.A. Boorman and I both obviously came from Europe and so from what can be called an outside world and I think that this is reflected in both of our movies. Similarly, Boorman and Marvin went on to work with each other again and also, of course, became friends. That is something that I am now myself experiencing with Ryan Gosling.

JW: *You and screenwriter Hossein Amini significantly expand Irene from the Sallis novel, providing the character with more of a back-story. Was this always your intention or did it become more of an imperative once Carey Mulligan expressed interest in the role?*

NWR: Carey Mulligan saw the character of Irene as a challenge, especially because she is sympathetic towards her husband, Standard, but also because she is irrevocably drawn to Driver, who becomes her knight in shining armour. Because of this kind of dual attraction it was a challenge to figure out with Hossein a way to make the love story work and to make sure that Irene wasn't just a small and incidental side character.

JW: *I note that the three car-chase sequences are each structured very differently. Each is precise and stylised, but unique from the other.*

NWR: The film fetishizes cars in most senses, from the obvious and almost parental care with which Shannon treats them through to Nino's equal regard for automobiles and I wanted to definitely carry this over into the car-chase sequences. Not only do these sequences vary from each other in the way that they are conceived and shot but they are scored differently too. I also wanted to have a lot of fun with these sequences even though they were each very meticulously planned and choreographed.

Another overriding principle was that I knew that I wanted to shoot at least one chase from the inside of the car. I really wanted to put the viewer in with the characters and give a sense of how close they could come at any moment to being killed. There was, of course, also with the sequences a need to demonstrate just how able and consummate Driver is. He is incredibly skilled and this is also shown in the moments where we see him at his 'day job' performing his stunt tricks. I also knew that I wanted one of the sequences to build incrementally; I liken it to a game of chess and the pitting of one man's wits against another's. The last sequence is a stalking sequence and is all about culminating in a stealth attack. It was all calculated to build to this last and quite sudden assault.

JW: *The film has moments of incredible violence and yet your presentation is discrete. You frequently favour sound over vision to convey brutality.*

NWR: I think that when violence comes it should always come as a shock and I don't think that violence, when presented in a film, should be lingered over in a pornographic manner. This was something I also very much wanted to avoid with *Bronson*, another of my works to focus on morally ambiguous central characters with a tendency towards psychosis, and I was very keen to insinuate and then do a quick reveal in *Drive* also. As you point out the sound was incredibly important, as was a focus upon suggestion and small yet significant detail. The example I tend to give is that of a few spots of blood on Driver's jacket rather than poring over in extreme detail the act that caused the blood spots to follow. In contrast to being pornographic I prefer to adopt an approach that could be labelled more soft-core. I think this is far more effective and also, to continue with the sexual metaphor, also more erotic. Filmmaking should be about the imagination and not necessarily what you see, but what you think you see.

JW: *I enjoyed the contrast between the flamboyant, hot-headed Nino [Ron Perlman] and the more reptilian and deceptive Bernie Rose [Albert Brooks].*

NWR: Besides being business partners they are childhood friends and though in many ways opposites have always been there for each other. They irritate each other but there is a definite bond. There is also a sense of mutual dependency. Nino is perhaps more dependent, hence the moment where Bernie has to kill Cook in Nino's Pizza place and turns to Nino saying: 'Now you can clean up after me for a change.'

JW: *In terms of a study of loneliness and solitude Walter Hill's* The Driver *[1978], Melville's* Le Samouraï *[1967] and Scorsese's* Taxi Driver *[1976] would seem to be antecedents. Were these films that you went back and looked at?*

NWR: I certainly spent a lot of time watching a lot of car-chase movies.

Kelly **Reichardt**

American landscapes and narratives of the road are the themes that run throughout the films of American filmmaker Kelly Reichardt.

Beginning her career with a number of arresting Super-8 shorts including *Then a Year* (2001) and *Travis* (2009), it was with *Ode* (1999), a reinterpretation of Herman Raucher's *Ode to Billy Joe* that Reichardt began a lasting collaboration with musician and actor Will Oldham.

Shot in her hometown of Dade Country, Florida, Reichardt's debut feature *River of Grass* (1994), a sun-drenched film noir was selected by both *Film Comment* and *The Village Voice* as one of the most accomplished features of its year.

Described as a New Age western, *Old Joy* (2006) saw Will Oldham relinquish soundtrack duties to Yo La Tengo but step in front of the camera in a beguiling account of contemporary masculinity and fractured friendships.

Again working from a story by Jon Raymond, *Wendy and Lucy* (2008) addresses issues of sympathy and generosity on the periphery of American life as it tracks the journey of Wendy Carroll and her dog Lucy to Alaska in search of lucrative summer work at a fish cannery. A portrait of a country in financial turmoil, it's an impeccable, poignant piece of cinema.

Since this interview Reichardt has reunited with *Wendy and Lucy* star Michelle Williams on the western travelogue *Meek's Cutoff* (2010) and more recently completed the political thriller *Night Moves* (2013) starring Jesse Eisenberg.

JASON WOOD: *I admired the organic feel of* Old Joy *and wondered if you and writer Jon Raymond followed a similar path for* Wendy and Lucy?

KELLY REICHARDT: We came up with a storyline together and then Jon wrote a short-story version called *Train Choir*. This is really where everything comes to light and the character is first flushed out. It's also when the environment and story take shape. Then I adapted his story to a script. We are always editing and contributing to whatever phase the writing is at but it's Jon that deals with the blank page that is really where the heavy lifting comes in. He also watches many of the final cuts of the film and gives me notes along the way.

JW: *Central to the film is the story of a struggle for self-sufficiency in contemporary America. How much did you want to reflect the current economic situation?*

KR: The seed of the idea of the story came just after the Katrina Hurricane hit and we were pondering this notion of how one can pull themselves up from their bootstraps if they don't have a social net or a decent education or any financial backing. We were also interested in this community of train-hopping kids – 'gutter punks' who are choosing to live off the grid, perhaps because they see no opportunities for themselves. These kids travel the country by hopping trains. It's quite a throw back, at least aesthetically, to the depression era of the 1930s.

JW: *Though you capture the natural beauty of the country there is also squalor to the malls and garages that reminded me of Jem Cohen's* Chain *[2004] in terms of corporate homogenisation. Was this also a subject with which you wished to engage?*

KR: *Chain* is such an amazing film. Yes, that was a concept that interested me. These places where she lands are familiar because they exist everywhere. That Walgreens parking lot is in every state and I'm sure it exists in her home state of Indiana, but at the same time there is no comfort in what's familiar because there is a soullessness to these spaces.

JW: *Your shorts and features never contain any extraneous material and everything seems very carefully calibrated. Is minimalism and economy something of a watchword for you?*

KR: It's just what is for me. It's the choice of story and the size of the productions and the pace I'm drawn to. It just seems to go that way.

JW: *In terms of the character of Wendy Carroll, you leave her history and her backstory open. Is it important for you that the spectator be allowed to form his or her own interpretations?*

KR: Yes. It's what I like most about Jon's writing – it allows the viewer to bring their

Wendy and Lucy, Kelly Reichardt, 2008 (Soda)

own ideas and experiences to the story. There's a lot of space and I think that's why it works well with my filmmaking.

JW: *Your work with actors is exemplary and it is great to see Will Oldham taking acting roles again after the intervening years since John Sayles'* Matewan *[1987]. How did you originally come across Oldham and after* Old Joy *how important to you was it that you again collaborate together?*

KR: Will has done a lot of acting between *Matewan* and *Old Joy*. Actually. He was in Phil Morrison's *Junebug* [2005] in the very opening scene. I met Will back when my first film *River of Grass* was out and he programmed it for a film night he was doing at a bar called Tonic in downtown New York. Then he did the soundtrack for my film *Ode* in 1998.

JW: *Wendy encounters quite a cross-section of characters. Some, despite worries of their own, are kind; others are pitiless and mean. One of the defining moments of the film is Walton Dalton's selfless financial gesture. How did you avoid such a moment spilling over into sentimentality?*

KR: Oh, there's a bit of sentiment there. It's hard not to feel sentimental about Walter in life or on the screen. But I think the way Michelle plays Wendy is key – she is not socially at ease ever and that helps to keep things from getting too mushy.

Ben **Rivers**

Ben Rivers studied Fine Art at Falmouth School of Art, initially in sculpture before moving into photography and Super-8mm film. After his degree, Rivers taught himself 16mm filmmaking and hand processing. His practice as a filmmaker treads a line between documentary and fiction, often following and filming people who have in some way separated themselves from society. His raw film footage provides Rivers with a starting point for creating oblique narratives imagining alternative existences in marginal worlds. *Sack Barrow* (2011) and *Slow Action* (2011) are two of his best-known shorter works.

The recipient of the FIPRESCI International Critics Prize at the 68th Venice Film Festival, *Two Years At Sea* (2011) is Rivers' debut feature. Extending the director's relationship with Jake, a man first encountered in *This Is My Land* (2006), the film follows a man who has chosen to live alone in a ramshackle house in the middle of the forest. Jake has a tremendous sense of purpose as he works around the house and surrounding forest and moorland, largely existing on the land and with only an old radio for company.

Rivers' witty and beautifully constructed film creates an intimate connection with an individual who might otherwise be hard to get to know if we met him face-to-face. A beguiling and frequently tempting portrait of a life lived without concession to consumer culture, it weaves an enticing and intoxicating spell.

―――――

JASON WOOD: *The film's title is quite oblique. Can you outline its significance?*

BEN RIVERS: *Two Years at Sea* refers to the time Jake spent working for a shipping company, all the while saving all his money to buy his dream property. He had been trying to get together with a group of friends to buy a shared property, but he told me it was too difficult to get everyone motivated and come to a shared decision, so he ended up saving for his own place. He was working between Britain and India, where he bought loads of cassette tapes with Indian music, which is what you hear in the film.

JW: *In terms of foregrounding could you explain your relationship with Jake Williams? What is it about Jake and his way of life that made you want to return to him for a feature-length piece?*

BR: *This Is My Land* was the first film in an ongoing series I've been making about people living off in the wilderness. It's a way of life that I've always been fascinated by, and had been trying to find someone to film back in 2005. Knut Hamsun's *Pan* sent me to northern Norway to try and find a similar character living in isolation, but I didn't find anyone and came back without a film. A friend then told me about Jake and that's how *This Is My Land* came about. It was the first film I'd made that employed documentary techniques, filming an actual person in their everyday setting, so for me it was a really important change in my filmmaking.

After that film, which was based very much in observation, I began to play around much more with this idea of what documentary means, and incorporating many more levels of construct into the films. Meanwhile, Jake had become a friend and also appeared in a road movie I made in 2009 called *I Know Where I'm Going*, where I travelled from London to the Isle of Mull, thinking about a post-human world. When I got the chance to make a feature-length film it just made sense to go back to him – because it had a nice circularity about it, and also because I always felt there was more to do at Jake's, that *This Is My Land* was just a sketch of sorts.

His life is very inspiring to me and there are seeming contradictions to that life which I find exciting; he is very ecologically aware and sensitive, and yet also has all this old machinery around; he really likes that landscape and environment, with its silence and birdsong, but also loves to blast out music into the forest. The other crucial reason I went back was because my filmmaking strategies had changed and I knew I wanted to exaggerate elements of his life, to fictionalise things to an extent. Because we were friends and Jake had liked *This is My Land* I knew that he would trust me to make something that didn't reflect badly on his way of life. If I had tried to make this film with someone I didn't know I think there would've been a much higher level of suspicion.

JW: *In terms of the actual process how did the shoot with Jake unfold in terms of the time you spent together and how much direction in terms of how he went about his day-to-day activities did you give him?*

Two Years at Sea, Ben Rivers, 2011 (Soda)

BR: I went up there five times over the course of a year, the first time by myself, and then all the other times with sound recordist Chu-Li Shewring; nobody else. We would spend about ten days up there each time, and this time wasn't all shooting. There's plenty of time to sit around chatting and eating, or helping Jake out with jobs. I didn't have a script, just a list of scenes I had in my head, such as: waking up; shower or bath; caravan; lake/raft; cooking and walking etc. I have images in my mind but these are open to change as soon as I'm looking through the camera. This to me is one of the exciting things about filmmaking, how events can change your preconceived ideas. Each day I usually had one or two goals, which we would try to achieve, though unexpected things can upset plans, particularly the weather.

Jake was an absolute professional. If I asked him if we could shoot something he was ready, and he didn't mind repeating things either. Almost all the shots in the film are set-up and directed in that we spent a lot of time together, and I could see what's going on there and get a sense of how best to shoot scenes. Then it's a matter of Jake kind of re-enacting himself for the camera, which he can do very naturally. Most action in the film is what he would do normally, apart from perhaps some of the more outlandish scenes, like the lake and the caravan up the tree.

JW: *There is an incredible sense of intimacy to the film. It's glimpse into the world and a life we would otherwise never know reminds me very much of Philip Trevellayn. Who were some of the influences?*

BR: I can't really remember if I was thinking about any other films specifically as I tend to shy away from this if I can, because when I first started making films many moons ago I was so beholden to other filmmakers that it was crippling. So I get stuck into my world and if I watch anything it tends to be very different, like trashy genre films. Whenever I got home to London after shooting I would spend quite a number of days processing the films in my kitchen. While I did this I could watch an episode of *Battlestar Gallactica* for each roll I developed. In the end I watched the whole series, but I'm not sure if it had an influence on the film other than I knew I didn't want to make anything like that. It was like a drug, I couldn't stop watching it even though I thought it was terrible.

JW: *It strikes me that an interest in figures who exist in some way outside of society, along with somewhat strange environments, is a recurring motif of your work. What is it about these topics that capture your imagination for you and where did these interests first develop?*

BR: They no doubt began to formulate in my childhood, growing up in a small village in Somerset, next to woods and a pretty ramshackle farm, not dissimilar to the one in my film *Ah, Liberty!* [2008]. The dichotomy of country and city has always been interesting for me, because I enjoy both, and being in one makes me yearn for the other. One of the great things about filmmaking is that it is a vehicle to go places and meet people, and all the people in my films are people I have enjoyed meeting and want to spend more time around. The spark is often related to their way of life, that they are doing things a bit differently, living in the wilderness and often fairly self-sufficient, but without being smug or judgemental towards the way other people live. As with Jake, there is usually a lot of junk and machine detritus around, and this coupled with the surrounding landscape is an important ingredient for me – the totems of technological society left scattered and degrading, ready to be re-used in some unforeseen way, or to disintegrate back into the landscape.

JW: *The film continues your tradition of favouring of different film stocks and hand-processing. What is it about this approach and the aesthetic effect it produces that appeals?*

BR: I think it goes hand-in-hand with the kinds of spaces I was just talking about – places that are not sanitised. There is roughness, dirt and unpredictability. When I make films I like encouraging different ways of not knowing what the final film will be, and using film can foster serendipity, especially when hand-processing, as there is always unknown qualities that occur. I always like watching the film back for the first time, sometimes weeks after it was filmed, and seeing how the processing leaves its mark on the material, like water marks or halos of light around objects caused by using developer too many times. For this film I really wanted to use Plus-X, one of my all-time favourite film stocks, which Kodak announced discontinuation of just after I began the film.

JW: *For me the two of the most striking elements of* Two Years at Sea *are the incredible black and white photography and the sense of silence that pervades throughout. What was your thinking in these regards?*

BR: The first time I went to Jake's for the feature I took both black and white and colour stock, and shot a bit of both. It was very clear when I got home and watched the material that the film should be in black and white. There was something about trying to show all the world in gradients of grey, and not cluttering it up more than necessary with colours. There's enough going on there already. I like thinking about the beginnings and ends of things, and humans, and somehow black and white fits with this. The film begins with the white of the snow and the white light of the projector, and ends with Jake's face disappearing into the blackness of the night and the blackness of cinema without light.

I love the silence of being in the middle of an evergreen forest, away from the noise of people. When I'm making a film I think about sound as much as the images I am making, so sound doesn't simply illustrate images but tries to get to a deeper sense of space. I'm interested in the idea of immersion in cinema, and sound can achieve this far more effectively than images. If an audience is willing then silence can be very powerful, and you can then attune your ear to more subtle occurrences, like when Jake is on the lake. It's really quiet and the distant sound of the grouse becomes an event. I also like disrupting the silence in the same way Jake does, often by blaring out music into the forest, because sometimes silence is oppressive.

JW: *The ending also has something immaculate about it. How difficult was it to achieve? Did you get through multiple tyres?*

BR: This shot had the most takes of the film, four. We made four fires, four tyres, very bad for the environment, but they burn brightly. We had shot three versions, all slightly different in length, and I was getting very black from standing right next to the fire. All three of us were feeling very tired as it was about 2am, and we sat by the dying embers with whiskeys, all dropping off to sleep. Suddenly and inexplicably I woke up and said we needed to do one more take, and I was right, the last one was the one which went in the film. Jake's face looks genuinely tired but also slightly amused. It's one of the most important shots in the film for me, one I had in mind pretty early on. In the end it's all you need, a long look at Jake's face as it merges with the grain of the film.

JW: *As a filmmaker whose work is considered to straddle the divide between fiction and documentary and whose work could be described as coming from a Fine Art and artists' cinema background, how do you feel that you are able to escape some of the rules of filmmaking and bring your own sensibility to bear on the medium?*

BR: Going to art school was a good start I think, in terms of not learning the rules in the first place. I visited some film schools after art school, but when I asked if I'd be able to do camera and direct they scoffed at me, which put me off, so I never went. It seemed better to learn from watching many films of all types, to get a sense of the multitudinous iterations cinema can take, which I did when some friends and I ran the cinema in Brighton. Perhaps most importantly, simply going into things and making mistakes can be the best way to develop, because sometimes those mistakes become very interesting tools. The collision between different modes of thinking and working always interests me, the spaces in-between things.

JW: *I also wondered how you found the transition from shorter pieces to the feature-length format of* Two Years at Sea?

BR: It wasn't a big leap, as my films had been getting steadily longer over the years. The actual process of making a feature wasn't really any different, apart from having a sound recordist there the whole time, which I had only done on one other film. Otherwise I worked the same way, only I just shot more.

JW: *Were you surprised at all by the fervour with which the film has been greeted? It had incredible screenings at Venice and the London Film Festival and also went on to enjoy success in cinemas as part of a theatrical release. What is it you feel that people are responding to? An alternative to the hubbub of modern living.*

BR: Perhaps it's that; a little quietness and reflection in times of insanity. Of course some folk found it a bit slow, but I think when audiences were open to go on the trip, to immerse themselves in this world, then it could offer something different to the usual cinema experience, which is so beholden to plot and exposition. My film doesn't stand alone either; there are other examples of contemporary filmmakers offering worlds that encourage more imagination on the part of the viewer, so that it's not just about taking in a narrative but asking for the audience to partake in completing the film. I was quite surprised it was released theatrically in the UK. And now it has been released in other countries. A black and white film with no dialogue.

JW: *What can you remember from your days programming the Brighton Cinematheque and what criteria did you employ in terms of your selections? I feel that UK audiences have been homogenised and have access to a far less diverse selection of cinema than they once did, more so outside metropolitan areas.*

BR: There are too many memories from those years. I can say though that our programming criteria was simply to show as much cinema, in all its many guises, that wasn't getting shown anywhere else. We started in 1996. The Scala was already over, and other great rep cinemas like the Everyman were already becoming way more conservative in their programming. We wanted to show everything from early cinema, through experimental cinema and trash underground features, to contemporary artist's cinema and rare repertory features. We also programmed expanded cinema and had live music. It was a lot of fun. Now I think there are less places that can do this – the Cube in Bristol and Star and Shadow in Newcastle are still going strong, but London is surprisingly lacking a regular space to show unusual films, and film projectors are disappearing, which limits some film programming because there's a lot of rare stuff out there unavailable on HD. Cinema is besieged. We have work to do.

Ira **Sachs**

Ira Sachs was born in Memphis in 1965. His first feature, *The Delta* (1997), enjoyed international festival acclaim.

With *Forty Shades of Blue* (2005) Sachs participated in the Screenwriter's Lab at the Sundance Institute. Set in the world of Memphis music, it confronts many of the issues that have been central to Sachs' work, most specifically characters who exist both inside and outside of their own environment.

The film is the story of Laura (Dina Korzun), a young Russian woman living in Memphis with a much older music legend (played by Rip Torn), and the personal awakening she experiences in the wake of her unfortunate affair with his estranged son. In the bars and bedrooms of this very contemporary city, a love triangle forms, illuminating the hearts and souls of these three tangled lives.

Sachs has since completed *Married Life* (2005) and the harrowing *Keep the Lights On* (2012), an exemplary tale of a contemporary gay relationship fuelled by addiction. Featuring the music of Arthur Russell, it is like *Forty Shades of Blue* (around which this interview is centred): a powerful, coruscating look at love in bad faith.

JASON WOOD: *I understand that genesis for* Forty Shades of Blue *was your relationship with your father.*

IRA SACHS: The film began with the idea to tell a story about a character that I knew growing up in my birthplace of Memphis. My parents divorced when I was eight and consequently my father, who was a larger-than-life business figure and man about town, had lots of girlfriends. As soon as I met one of these girlfriends I would have an antagonistic relationship with them as they were different from me and were frequently from different classes, backgrounds and experiences.

Strangely, I have since gotten to know some of these women who have stayed in my life over twenty or thirty years. The actual characters in the film are very different from the ones that I knew but the plot and the trajectory is pretty much the same. I think the film is about that process of going underneath and getting to know someone that you might dismiss in your first meeting. It is about looking a little harder and listening a little bit more. You do this in film too; you look at characters that initially seem peripheral. I've always done this when watching films and also in my own work, such as my previous feature *The Delta*. It's a fascination with characters on the outside. I remember watching *Straight Time* [1978] and thinking rather than a film about the Dustin Hoffman character wouldn't it be interesting to have a film about the character played by Theresa Russell?

JW: *Laura, played by Dina Korzun, certainly starts on the periphery, moving to the centre through a process of self-discovery.*

IS: I've always been compelled by female characters and love novels by writers such as Edith Wharton and Henry James – *Portrait of a Lady* and *House of Mirth* especially. I also love the films of Fassbinder and Buñuel's *Belle de Jour* [1967] and Godard's *Contempt* [1963], pictures where women take on a central role that is somehow larger than the director. You must have the right actress in this position because quite often these roles are not particularly verbal, but come from the character's interior strength. We were very conscious of how we developed Laura and if you look closely you'll notice that she has seventeen different looks throughout the film to define her visually, psychologically and in narrative terms. I had pictures of Catherine Deneuve and Monica Vitti on my wall as guides, pictures of women who moved through films with an iconic presence. Even though the film is quite naturalistic in its approach I also knew that this was going to be a film that would be very much crafted. It's the craft that makes the audience relax a little. They will know that they are watching something that has been crafted for them and they can relax and experience it in a different way.

My grandmother, an outsider who came to Memphis from New York, also influenced me. Nobody ever really understood her. Laura's habit of saying 'pretty good' whenever Alan asks her how she is doing is actually something my grandmother would say. She was somehow out of step with her society.

Forty Shades of Blue, Ira Sachs, 2005 (Artificial Eye)

This is something I could personally relate to. Growing up gay in Memphis takes a little bit of time to figure out. I am certainly compelled by characters that are on the outside for this reason and it is no coincidence that in this film and in *The Delta* the central characters are immigrants. It's a translation of that experience of being out of step with where we are.

JW: *What made you cast Dina Korzun?*

IS: I knew that casting was essential and the most important job I had as the film is defined by the shades and the details in every beat. I saw Dina in *Last Resort* [2000] and after meeting her was struck by her combination of naturalism and classical training. Dina brings a density to the performance that really carries the film. I had to really track her down actually and came here to London to meet her. She has a very intelligent approach to constructing her character and steered the film away from being a purely observational drama. I was really impressed by just how conscious she is of being able to create effect and emotion for the audience.

JW: *Did you write Alan James with Rip Torn in mind?*

IS: I wrote the part for Rip because as an actor and as a man of the world he is similar to the type of character we were writing, a powerful man with an earthy combination of expressiveness and poetry. Alan James is also based on producers including Sam Phillips of Sun Records, Willie Mitchell, Al Green's producer, and Jim Dickinson who produced Big Star and who also played piano on the Stones' 'Wild Horses'. These people were kings of their domain, and they were brilliant. Rip has this too. He's complicated and volatile, but also extremely sensitive and human. Even though his character is being heralded for bringing glory to Memphis, there is a sense that in domestic terms he is vulnerable. I think that by the end of the film you have a very clear sense that this man is mortal. Rip approached the part as if it was King Lear and to do Lear well you have to have a sense of comedy and tragedy. Rip knows how to make light what could otherwise be very heavy. He is the oldest person in the film at 74 but he brings an energy to it that drives everyone else.

JW: *Memphis becomes its own character.*

IS: It's a city that I know really well and in a way that is instinctual and impressionistic. It's an active city where things happen but where the inhabitants are not particularly verbal. I wanted to tell a domestic melodrama within that environment and to do so I was able to use all these great locations because of my relationship with the place. We shot in locations including the Peabody Hotel and Ardent Studios, which is where all the Big Star albums were recorded.

A lot of the background faces are also Memphis characters, such as Charles 'Skip' Pitts who played the original guitar lick on *Shaft*. I think the fact that I paid this attention gives authenticity to the depiction of the city. It's about getting information into the frame so that people feel that they are experiencing something with depth. On the other hand I had some financiers who had just seen *Lost in Translation* (2003) and I think they wanted me to shoot *Lost In Memphis*. They wanted me to shoot the river and have every element of the city in the film. I had to argue to maintain a less fetishistic approach to the city of Memphis.

JW: *And what was your visual approach to the city?*

IS: I wanted a vivid approach that was not entirely defined by colour. I looked at lots of show reels of DP's who had worked on credible indie movies and although their work was very decent nothing stood out and convinced me that they would be right for this film. I found Julian Watley who ended up shooting the film by poring over endless show reels and coming across a video that he shot for Green Day's 'Time of Your Life'. There was a sense that here was someone who could use natural light to a transformative effect. Within a short sequence I was able to see someone who could capture the elements of the everyday and turn them into something else. Julian and I met and I discovered that he had worked as a camera operator for David Fincher but had never shot a feature before so there was an element of risk for both of us. It was a process of trying to translate what were my impressions of a certain shooting style that I was coming to and then for Julian to find a way to achieve that on a technical and impressionistic level. We used three Ken Loach films as templates: *Kes* [1969], *Family Life* [1999] and *Looks and Smiles* [1981]. It was photojournalism filtered though Nan Goldin. If you froze any frame you would see a clear aesthetic choice.

Céline **Sciamma**

A coming-of-age tale set amidst the world of synchronised swimming, Céline Sciamma's sensitive and perceptive debut, *Water Lilies* (2007) captures the pleasure and pain of teenage life as three fifteen-year-old girls explore their burgeoning sexuality.

Unfolding over a languid summer in an anonymous Parisian suburb it begins with Marie's (Pauline Acquart) hopes of making her local synchronised swimming team. An ambition founded on a sexual attraction towards the team's popular captain, Floriane (Adèle Haenel), Marie finds herself becoming an accomplice in a series of uncomfortable assignations with Floriane's boyfriend, François. Marie's best friend Anne (Louise Blachére) also has François in her sights. As friendships fray Sciamma sets the stage for a series of power struggles.

A tender drama but with flashes of humour, Sciamma confidently explores territory previously occupied by Catherine Breillat and Lucrecia Martel. The spirit of Esther Williams also lingers in the distinctive underwater scenes. Bold, visually assured and knowingly kitsch, *Water Lilies* is all the more impressive for being Sciamma's first ever foray behind the camera. She followed it with the equally accomplished *Tomboy* (2011).

JASON WOOD: *The fact that you had never made even a short before directing your first feature has become a source of keen interest.*

CÉLINE SCIAMMA: I consider it a chance that I've been given. It was an incredible opportunity to strongly affirm my beliefs and style. The approach was fresh for me and for the audience as everybody, including myself, was going to discover my vision. The fact that everything went so fast – I shot the movie few months after I wrote it – allowed me to ask myself nothing but questions of work. I had no time to wonder about being legitimate, or fantasising about being a director. I had to do it.

JW: *Was the decision to set the film within the world of synchronised swimming based on any personal experience and what was it about that world that captured your attention?*

CS: When I was fifteen I attended by chance a synchronised swimming exhibition. The emotion that struck me at the time was very strange. I thought I had missed my vocation and that I should have been a synchronised swimmer. There was also the fact that those girls were so accomplished; they were so feminine while I was still childish in appearance and they were part of a team while I felt alone. I thought that absurd anecdote was truly a great example of the confusion you feel at that time of life, when you are confused by your desires.

Writing the film I took a deeper interest in the sport, hanging around at competitions every weekend. The thing that interests me mostly in this world is the what it says about the girls' condition. Synchronised swimmers are soldiers who look like dolls. On the surface they have to pretend that they don't suffer, whereas underneath they struggle painfully. It reveals a lot about the job of being a girl.

JW: *You offer a uniquely female perspective on your three teenage protagonists and in talking about women avoid the male fantasy so common to films dealing with archetypal female issues. I know that you are keen that the film not be promoted under a specific banner but was this depiction of 'how tough it is to be a girl' one of your primary objectives?*

CS: It was definitely the primary objective. Even before I had the storyline, I knew that I wanted to depict what I call 'the difficult job of being a girl'. Cinema has been talking about women for a century now but men have mostly done the talking. I wanted to go against the folklore of teenage girls in cotton underwear and their mysteries. I wanted the film to be an answer to that undying tradition of fascination. *Water Lilies* goes into the locker rooms of girls not to fantasise but to see the crude reality.

JW: *Equally striking is the lack of an adult perspective.*

CS: I started writing scenes with the parents of the young characters, but I quickly found it boring. Relationships between teenagers and adults is a complex and subtle subject and it exists at the heart of the French tradition of teen movies from *Les quatre cents coups* [1959] to *Á nos amours* [1983]. I decided that I'd rather not talk about it at all and dispensed with this aspect after the first draft. It's also because I wanted everyone in the audience to identify with a fifteen-year-old girl. Adult characters could have allowed the audience to find refuge elsewhere. That wasn't the experience and the journey I wanted the audience to take. I also didn't want to talk about teenage boys so rather than doing it superficially I decided not to do it at all.

JW: *Where did you shoot and why did you avoid placing the film in a specific moment in time?*

CS: We shot in Cergy, a new town thirty miles from Paris. It's an experimental town that was born at the end of the 1960s. I chose it because it's visually very interesting; it's France, yet it could be the suburbs of North America. It has a strong visual and architectural identity that encouraged stylisation.

I desperately wanted to avoid placing the film in a specific moment for several reasons. Teen movies frequently portray youth at a specific moment and that I didn't want to do. I wanted to portray universal and undying feelings and sensations. I didn't want to do a generational movie that would be an inside look on the teenagers of 2006. So I got rid of contemporary teenage folklore. Also, I didn't want a nostalgic look at that period of life so I didn't set it in the past. I wanted everyone to be welcome in the movie; it's the emotions I wanted to be in the present time.

JW: *Water Lilies is especially impressive in its depiction of the awakening of Marie's desires.*

CS: I didn't want to adopt a sociological approach. I like to think that homosexuality is not a subject but a journey. I wanted to observe a very small moment: the awakening of the desire, the journey of that desire from the moment it is born in the stomach until it travels to Marie's consciousness. As a matter of fact, *Water Lilies* ends where most films concentrating on homosexual desire begin. I wanted to capture this birth of desire, rather than its affirmation.

JW: *How did you come to cast Pauline Acquart, Louise Blachère and Adèle Haenel and how did you work with them to prepare them for their roles?*

CS: We'd been looking everywhere for the three girls: in the streets, in high schools and in shopping malls. We found them in three different ways. Pauline was spotted by the casting director in a public garden; Louise answered an ad we had put in a magazine and Adèle had already been in a feature film when she was a child. We worked together for a month prior to shooting with the help of a coach. It was mostly a matter of trust and honesty between us. I didn't want to be a puppet master with my young cast. I wanted them to be very aware of what we were going to tell together. I wanted them to be engaged in the movie. That's why I wanted them to be the same age as the girls they were playing. I knew that they would feel responsible toward the subject of the film. I put them in charge; they were going to be spokeswomen for the girls' condition!

JW: *What has been the most positive outcome of making* Water Lilies?

CS: There's been nothing but positive outcomes surrounding the film: the Cannes film festival, the French release that triggered the interest of the press and the audience… The thing that I'm really proud of is the fact that the movie is having an international career. It has travelled a lot and met a lot of very different audiences. I like the fact that it comes from France but has developed a multicultural identity.

Peter **Strickland**

Reading-born writer-director Peter Strickland's first feature film *Katalin Varga* (2009) was made entirely independently over a four-year period. It went on to win many awards including a Silver Bear in Berlin and the European Film Academy's Discovery of the Year award.

Prior to this, Strickland made a number of short films including *Bubblegum* (1996) and *A Metaphysical Education* (2004). He also founded the Sonic Catering Band, releasing several records and performing live throughout Europe. The band also released field recordings, sound poetry and modern classical music in very limited vinyl editions.

Berberian Sound Studio (2012) saw him return with a very different but no less unique vision. A timid sound engineer (played by Toby Jones) arrives in Italy to work on a mysterious horror film, mixing bloodcurdling screams with the grotesque sounds of hacked vegetables. But as the onscreen violence seeps into his consciousness reality and fantasy become blurred and a nightmare begins.

Daringly original and masterfully constructed, this inspired homage to 1970s Italian *giallo* horror is a cineastes' fantasy. A devastating assault on the senses, it is quite unlike anything else in recent British cinema. The closest comparison I can think of is *Peeping Tom* (1960).

JASON WOOD: *How did the idea for* Berberian Sound Studio *begin to form?*

PETER STRICKLAND: It began as a joke when I made it as a one-minute film with the Bohman Brothers in 2005. Then it came to life again a few years later when I thought about the stories behind some of the *giallo* soundtracks. Some of those soundtracks were very advanced for the time with their use of drone, musique concrète, free jazz and dissonance. The music of Bruno Maderna, Ennio Morricone and Gruppo di Improvisazione Nuova Consonanza existed in the same high-art camp as Stockhausen, Cage or AMM, but then these guys were making money on the side composing soundtracks for B-grade horror films. *Berberian Sound Studio* came out of that strange, sonic no man's land between academia and exploitation. What's interesting about so many of those horror soundtracks along with the sound design is that people who turn their noses up at that genre would probably love the music and sound taken out of context. The same goes for people who don't like 'difficult' music – in the context of horror, people get Penderecki. I think I remember Stereolab's Tim Gane saying in an interview how the horror genre can warm people up to sonic ideas they wouldn't find palatable in a recorded context. *The Texas Chainsaw Massacre* [1974] is a really good example of phenomenally crafted musique concrète that many people, sadly, wouldn't accept out of its horror context.

The script just swam around that idea, but also incorporating foley and overdubs. I guess I was attracted by how something unspeakably horrific can be so ridiculous once you take it to a foley stage. As an audience, you're caught between the sound of a woman being murdered and the sight of a man flapping cabbages. The two things are as far removed as you can get and I wanted to focus on an innocent man surrounded by colleagues who have been doing this for years and who are completely blasé about the horror they witness.

I also wanted to make something visually quite innocent, but aurally very unpleasant. Maybe subconsciously I was inspired by one or two videos I wasn't allowed to see as a teenager. I could hear the screaming and sound effects from a video my older brother and his friends watched on one occasion. I was too young to be allowed to watch it, so I just stood outside the door and listened. That probably has a lot to do with how I got to this film.

I don't want to come across as too 'art school', but when you deal with the illusion of violence, you're inevitably making a reflexive piece of work that questions both an audience's consumption of it and how filmmakers represent it. The main challenge was whether filmmakers can responsibly portray violence without sensationalising it. It's a very tough question: no matter how high-minded you are as a filmmaker in terms of seriously portraying violence, you can't control the interpretation of your images once they reach an audience. In some ways, that's why I respect some of the *giallo* directors. There's an honesty about exploitation. When some directors comment on how they wanted to show how terrible it is when someone is tortured or whatever, it either smacks of bullshit or folly. That kind of hypocritical attitude is shown in the film, but I hope I'm being more satirical than didactic.

As the script started to shape up, other things crept in. Nepotism, corruption and just general things I either saw or experienced over the years, but unless you're going to devote a whole film to those subjects, it's better not to emphasise them too much. But ultimately, the one thing that excited me the most was just messing around with sound. It doesn't have much to do with effects, more to do with the power of sound to confound and deceive.

JW: *The film's interest in sound reminded me of* The Conversation *[1974] and* Blow Out *[1981]. Could you talk about some of your interests and inspirations?*

PS: We took a few cues from some *giallo* films, but the film within the film fed more off the Gothic horror of Bava's *Black Sunday* [1969] or Argento's *Suspiria* [1977]. Music played a big part in how I thought about the film. It goes without saying that Italian horror soundtracks were essential (Morricone, Bruno Nicolai, Riz Ortolani, Stelvio Cipriani, Fabio Frizzi, Claudio Gizzi, Goblin), but there were so many ideas in records by Luc Ferrari, the Bohman Brothers, Cathy Berberian, Katalin Ladik, Jean-Michel Van Schouwburg, Luigi Nono, Jim O'Rourke, Nurse with Wound, Faust, Merzbow, Trevor Wishart, early Whitehouse, early Franco Battiato and Broadcast, of course. The influence of all that music is felt throughout the film. Even the studio photographs found in some of the Battiato or Gruppo di Improvisazione Nuova Consonanza albums gave clues to the atmosphere and look of the film.

In terms of film, the biggest influence was *The Cremator* [1969] by Juraj Herz. Superficially there is no resemblance, but the way Herz edited some of the scenes in that film was a template for us. I also got into Peter Tscherkassky in a big way. I thought avant-garde film had lost its way in the 1990s, but Tscherkassky came along and completely split the atom. Both structurally and visually, we are paying tribute to those filmmakers or just plainly ripping them off depending on your point of view.

JW: *The design elements are impeccable. How did you achieve the look and feel of the film? I am thinking especially of the attention to detail of the tape titles and the general way in which design is used. Who were your collaborators?*

PS: One of the reasons I wanted to write about analogue sound is because it was so incredibly visual both in terms of the machinery and the performance aspect of splicing tape and looping it. You look at those old control rooms and they do have a very powerful, otherworldly feel: the racks full of oscillators, filters and oscilloscopes; the tape boxes and dubbing charts. There's a ritualistic and mysterious quality to it all and the film is meant to celebrate that. With digital, there's nothing mysterious about watching someone clicking on their plug-ins.

The studio itself is a composite of different studios I visited in Hungary and the Studio di Fonologia in Milan where some of the most interesting music happened. Cathy Berberian, Luciano Berio, Bruno Maderna, Marino Zuccheri and Luigi Nono all made incredible stuff there. We threw in a long Luigi Nono sample into the film to make the nod more explicit.

Jennifer Kernke, the production designer did a great job of assimilating all those influences and making something that took the best bits out of all the studios referenced. The only problem we had was sourcing the equipment. I wanted every piece of equipment in the mixing room to be the same as in the Fonologia studio, but it was a pointless exercise even if one travelled to Italy. We ended up with some Bruel & Kjaer 1011 oscillators that were faithful to the original rack list that an Italian acquaintance compiled, but stuff like two-ring modulators and the General Radio 1398-A tone burst generator were bloody hard to find. Most of that equipment has disappeared. The curse of digital is that sound engineers now find it acceptable to throw an AEG Telefunken reel-to-reel into a skip.

When it came to the tape boxes and papers, we approached Julian House. I was familiar with his record designs for Broadcast and other bands, but his own Ghost Box record label had this very arcane sensibility, which was tapping into similar territory. He instantly knew what was needed for the film and often led the way, pushing the design aspect more in the direction it had to go in. He had the idea of coming up with a fake title sequence for the film within the film, which I thought was brilliant. We spoke about the title sequence to *The Cremator* as a loose influence for what he would do, but otherwise he went off and did everything himself. I supplied him with some photos of two Slovak girls screaming, which was a salute of sorts to Herz's home country.

Julian designed the Berberian logo, the tape boxes and the dubbing charts amongst other things. We could have used existing boxes, but thought it better to make up our own brands from scratch both for Gilderoy's home 'Shears Magnetic' tapes and the Italian studio 'Ventri Fonologia' tapes.

The dubbing charts are there for atmosphere and 'look' as much as information about the process of the film within the film. It took a lot of time to fill them in and it all had to be shot after the main shoot on a special 'paperwork' day several months later. It also took weeks to find the right paper to print Julian's template on, but it paid off. Even though it doesn't matter if one can't follow the charts, it was important for every single number and word to make sense for anyone who would know how to read them. I probably made a mistake somewhere along the line with the numbering, but the intention was there.

There is one abstract score included by a guy called Krisztián Kristóf, which was inspired by the notational scores drawn by Iannis Xenakis and Trevor Wishart. It goes back to the ritualistic aspect of soundmaking. You look at these scores and wonder if there is some hidden pagan message within them. You can see why Joe Meek and Graham Bond lost it with black magic.

JW: *Sound and music has always been essential to you. Can you talk about your general approach to sound and also how Broadcast came to be involved in the soundtrack.*

PS: The initial temptation with this film was to drench it in all manner of sonic effects and trickery. There would have been creative licence to do that since we're making a film about sound, but it might have been self-defeating. It felt more appropriate to hold the scope of the sound back and focus more on detail and perspective. When you're dealing with tape machines, headphones, loudspeakers and so on, there's a lot of fun to be had in constantly shifting the sonic pers-pective whilst remaining completely naturalistic. On one or two occasions, we cheated, but as a general rule, all the sound in the film, including the music, is diegetic. Everything you hear is physically present coming from a machine, instrument or whatever else is in the room. Since the narrative is a little askew, it's quite important to at least anchor the film in a sonic reality. Nothing comes from a character's head and certainly nothing is laid on the soundtrack by the sound team. There isn't a soundtrack as such and the closest you get to being in Gilderoy's head is when he has his headphones on and we just amplify what's in there. But in general, we tried to be spare with the sound and not overuse effects. What took the most time was making the different sonic perspectives seem believable.

The screams took a lot of time as well, but most of that was done before the shoot. We tried to amass as many screams as we could from friends or some of the cast and then send it to various soundmen I knew who could make everything more aggressive or abstract. Andrew Liles gave me two CDs filled with treated screams and after a while it started to mess with my head. I started to see how someone could go bananas listening to this stuff every day. Suzy Kendall from *The Bird with the Crystal Plumage* [1970], *Torso* [1973] and *Spasmo* [1974] came in to scream for the film and told me some very funny stories about her *giallo* days. She did all the screams for *The Bird with the Crystal Plumage*, so it felt like a blessing to have her with us.

Broadcast were my only choice for this film. They used to talk about Basil Kirchin and Bruno Nicolai in interviews and just from those two names, all I had to do was join the dots. They knew all the influences inside out and had a way of summoning that sound from the past without falling into pastiche. Their former keyboardist, Roj did some sounds for *Katalin Varga*, so he put me in touch with Trish and James around September 2009, but it wasn't until 2010 when we started to properly talk about the soundtrack and what should and shouldn't be done. I started off by talking about the more obvious references, but they quickly got

Berberian Sound Studio, Peter Strickland, 2012 (Wild Horses/BFI/BBC)

me on the right track by playing me very obscure but beautiful records from that period. A few tracks were sent in advance of the shoot, but most of the music came in during the edit period and it was a back and forth process right up until the very last day of sound mixing, but everything mostly took shape during the edit with Chris Dickens.

Speaking purely as a fan of the band, Trish's passing is a huge loss. It's not an overstatement to say that she was one of the most remarkably gifted musicians of my generation.

JW: *How was the experience of working with Toby Jones?*

PS: Toby fully immersed himself in the character and got there pretty quickly in terms of the stillness within Gilderoy. It's a very hard thing to carry a film yet remain believably nondescript, but he pulled it off very well. He's not a 'broad stroke' actor. He did small things that I barely noticed on set, but when you see it on the big screen, those little gestures reveal a whole inner life. He had already done a radio play that involved foley, so this wasn't that unfamiliar to him.

As with anyone you work with, you have your good days and bad days, but that's not a big deal. In hindsight, I probably should've spent more time talking to Toby and the other actors than constantly trying to get the correct wave pattern on the oscilloscope. It doesn't matter now. On screen, Toby is more Gilderoy than the Gilderoy I initially had in my head, so I have nothing but praise for him.

JW: *I was intrigued by the device of the letters from home. It hints at a world beyond what we see on screen and a strange relationship between the Toby Jones character and his mother...*

PS: The letters are an extension of the film within the film idea in that once again you are denied the sight of that other world, but this time instead of extreme horror, it's the tranquillity of Gilderoy's back garden in Dorking, which you only see once in a photograph. The letters are there to set up Gilderoy's world, but also to offer clues to later scenes. Both the letters and Gilderoy's home recordings start to intersect with the horror film, but there's a loneliness and silence there for me that puts the whole film within the right frame.

Gilderoy himself is a composite of a few people I know, but he also harks back to the days of the garden-shed sound eccentric. I had this romantic idea of the artisan sound eccentric working away in the garden shed. Even if they didn't work in sheds, you can imagine that could be the only place where Vernon Elliott or Desmond Leslie made their recordings.

I don't know why I chose Dorking. I just imagined there'd be many garden sheds there. The more I visited the town, the more it became the only place where Gilderoy could have come from. There were a few very pleasant moments of 'synchronicity' there. The weirdest thing was when I went to photograph a garden shed. After making a few calls in Dorking, I found this man who agreed to have his shed photographed for the film and after telling him a little about the film, it turned out he was a fan of the Ghost Box label, which made me feel it was right to make the effort rather than sourcing a shed image online.

JW: *Despite the tribulations you faced in completing* Katalin Varga *it was very well received. How did making your second feature compare and how would you contrast the two experiences?*

PS: Not an easy one to answer. If I could go back in time, I wouldn't have made *Katalin Varga*. The emotional and financial toll it took was too much. It's a vile memory apart from those few weeks of shooting, which were very beautiful in hindsight. If I think about comparing the shoots only, they are worlds apart. Almost all of *Berberian* was shot in Three Mills Studio in London. I had never even been in a studio before and it was a little intimidating at first. Eventually, I got the idea that all these crewmembers are not on set to break my balls, but to make my life easier.

The accommodation near Three Mills was luxurious but soulless. At least I didn't have to share a bed with my cameraman this time, which might explain why I got on better with Nic than with Mark, my previous cameraman. Saying that, part of me misses the chaos of the *Varga* sleeping arrangements. There's a comfort to be had in the snoring around you.

When we shot *Varga* in Transylvania, it was very slow on the one hand because you just got caught up in mundane dramas with the farmers and their livestock, but when we had the chance to shoot, we could move very fast. A camera, tripod and reflector and that was it. No lights, rigs or tracks to worry about. *Berberian* was time-consuming because it's naturally so fiddly in the studio removing walls and so on when we want to change angle, but at least I didn't have to worry about ticks crawling up my ankles. Endless differences – good and bad things about both shoots.

JW: *What kind of reaction are you hoping for in regard to* **Berberian***? Are you expecting adulation, confusion, trepidation or a combination of all of these?*

PS: I have no idea what to expect. No idea whatsoever. The most important thing is the film was made the way it needed to be made without second-guessing what an audience would respond to. As long as one is true to that, something will work out OK even if it's not in the short-term.

It's not important to get all the references or understand everything. It's a film that's meant to be experienced much in the same manner as a piece of music. As long as an audience can go into this by losing themselves in another world, then the chances are they won't ask for a refund.

Tilda **Swinton**

Tilda Swinton is many things but she is not a film director. As such, she stands apart from the rest of the interviewees in this book. However, from interviewing Swinton for the release of Lynne Ramsay's *We Need To Talk About Kevin* (2011) it became transparently clear that she is very much a driving force behind many of the films that she makes and that her bond with her directors goes beyond that of merely muse or hired hand.

A striking and distinctive presence onscreen and off, Swinton's career began with close collaborations with Derek Jarman. It was a creative partnership that would last until Jarman's death in 1994. For the maverick director Swinton appeared in *Caravaggio* (1986), his segment of *Aria* (1987), *The Last of England* (1988), *War Requiem* (1989), *The Garden* (1990), *Edward II* (1991), *Wittgenstein* (1993), and lent her voice to his final film *Blue* (1993).

Seeking out directors whose work existed outside of the mainstream, Swinton also appeared in Peter Wollen's *Friendship's Death* (1987), as the gender-swapping title character in Sally Potter's *Orlando* (1992) and in Lynn Hershman Leeson's time-spanning fantasy *Conceiving Ada* (1997). Swinton then excelled as the foul and abusive Muriel Belcher in John Maybury's Francis Bacon biopic *Love is the Devil* (1998) and as the mother of a teenage daughter forced into an incestuous relationship in Tim Roth's controversial *The War Zone* (1999).

From Danny Boyle's *The Beach* (2000) onwards Swinton has been able to balance roles in more mainstream fare with her championing of independent productions. Thus, for every *The Curious Case of Benjamin Button* (2008) and *Michael Clayton* (2007), for which Swinton won a Best Supporting Actress Academy Award, there is a *Young Adam* (2003) and *The Man From London* (2007) for recently retired Hungarian auteur Béla Tarr.

An adaptation of Lionel Shriver's novel of the same name, *We Need To Talk*

About Kevin witnesses perhaps Swinton's most remarkable performances to date as the mother of a psychotic son with extremely violent tendencies.

———

JASON WOOD: *You had been talking to Lynne Ramsay about collaborating on a film adaptation of Lionel Shriver's novel for some time. What was it about the novel and working with Lynne that excited you?*

TILDA SWINTON: I never quite know if I'd have been as interested in the book were I not a mother when I read it but let's just say I would have been. I was certainly the child of a mother when I read it. The thing that that struck me as clear when I read it is that Lionel Shriver is looking at stuff that is unsayable or unsaid about the realities of the maternal instinct not being inevitable. That was always going to be of interest to me because she is entering a molten territory of people not knowing how to be people and mothers not knowing how to be mothers. I had had children by the time I read the novel and I was aware of two things the second I had them. The first was how much I was into them the moment I saw them and the second was how I was suddenly aware of how it might have gone a different way. That was striking to me. Before having children it had never occurred to me that it might have been different but I was filled with a gratitude that the chemical reaction was happening for me. When I read the book I realised that Lionel had articulated her instinct about this, not even her experience which is another of the reasons why it is so impressive, that she pulled that corner of the carpet up and was looking right underneath it.

Like most people who have seen a Lynne Ramsay film I was eagerly awaiting the next one and so after I'd met her and we had become friends I was keen to help Lynne in any way to make her own film. It wasn't actually clear to either of us that I would be actually in her next film. The place Lynne occupies in cinema is similar in some respects to what I am talking about regarding Lionel Shriver. I think Lynne is really at ease with people at a point of great discomfort. I was really happy to go with Lynne into that area and as this book also occupies this territory it's a very good match.

JW: *The film features a high school massacre and yet one of its most original features is that it concentrates less on this and more on the subject of disconnected parenting. Was this appealing to you given that recent films such as* Elephant *[2003] and* Polytechnique *[2009] had explored similar terrain?*

TS: As far as I am concerned that is exactly what the film is about. To my mind this film has as much to do with the practical nature of parenting as *Rosemary's*

Baby [1968] is about the practical business of being pregnant. It's a fantasy. The woman in *Rosemary's Baby* – and us the audience – fantasise about Rosemary being impregnated by the Devil. The fact that she actually is is beside the point. It's about the worst-case scenario growing inside of her and inside of us as the audience. The fact that Kevin becomes a killer at the end is not the worst part of this story at all. There are worse horrors in the heart of this film. For me the violence of the film is more in Eva's incapacity to meet Kevin or to engage with him. For me one of the most violent moments of the film is what I call the 'is this about fucking?' scene where Eva is telling Kevin that she is going to have another baby and that he'll get used to it and Kevin replies that 'just because you get used to something it doesn't mean that you like it. You're used to me.' And when we cut back to her she does this unimaginable thing for a mother in that she doesn't leap to reassure him. In fact she doesn't do anything other than to say 'well, yeah in a few weeks we're going to get used to someone else'. This moment is so violent.

There is actually very little physical violence in this film. There's actually hardly any blood except for a little bit of wound blood that you see on the bodies being wheeled out of the gym. You see hardly any violence being perpetrated at all. What you actually see is absence, an absence of engagement, an absence of reassurance; an absence of feeling and that is perhaps the most violent thing of all. The high school massacre was always going to be the least interesting aspect of this territory.

JW: *One of the other fascinating things about Eva is the fact that she set aside her ambitions and her career to give birth to Kevin. She was talented and ambitious…*

TS: And she still is.

JW: *She has to put her talent and ambition on hold to have a connection with Kevin. I'm not sure that I'd describe her as resentful but do you see this as the source of the blockade between Eva and Kevin?*

TS: I would put your point more sharply. That's why I wanted to interrupt you. She still is talented and ambitious and she is kyboshed by this pregnancy and her denial of the sacrifice that parenthood inevitably brings about is absolute. We can't pussyfoot around this. Eva is in a major sulk about it and her feelings in this regard are violent. The fact is that she is in denial about it and the fact is that Kevin picks this up. How could he not? I don't want to over-psychoanalyse the film, in fact that is something that I am very keen to avoid, but it needs to be said that Eva is faking it, majorly. Franklin is too. At one point Lynne and I were fantasising about alternative titles for the film when we didn't want to call it the name

We Need To Talk About Kevin, Lynne Ramsay, 2011 (Independent/Artificial Eye)

of the book and we fantasised about calling it *Performance*. There is, of course, already a great film of that title and in many ways both films are about fakery and façade. Franklin constantly adopts a 'Hey buddy' school of fatherhood, which must be infuriating. Eva is doing an 'I want to be in France but I'm not going to tell anybody' act and so it's actually very hard not to sympathise with Kevin. He's super-bright. How could he not notice any of this?

JW: *In an interview from Cannes, Ezra Miller spoke of Franklin's refusal to acknowledge the darkness as being the core of the problem.*

TS: This must be even more disturbing for Kevin than the behaviour of his mother. As the testosterone holder in the household Franklin is really dropping the ball. You can take it even further and this perhaps refers more to the book than it does to the film but you can look at what Lionel Shriver has to say about society and Bush-era American society and particularly the privileged milieu society this family exists within. Another fantasy title for me was *Peacetime* because we are all supposed to be living in this era of peace and look at what has just happened in Norway [Anders Behring Breivik massacred 77 people in a bomb attack in Oslo and a shooting spree at a youth camp on the island of Utoya on 22 July 2011].

JW: *In some ways* We Need To Talk About Kevin *reminds me of* The War Zone, *one of your earlier films that deals with conflict but locates it within a family.*

TS: I suppose they both deal with the violence of the real. Violence seems to be one of the most explicit ways to get people to focus. The Greeks knew this, hence their dedication to cathartic drama. We spoke a lot about this film being a Greek tragedy. It's a Greek tragedy more than anything. This, and budgetary constraints, is why the violence takes place off-screen. We also have a very limited number of protagonists and we also have a chorus, the people outside of the school. But the Greek tragedy does involve a kind of maelstrom of nonsense, encompassing Eva's weird disconnect and Franklin's aforementioned 'Hey buddy' act.

I think that another tragic element of this story is that in many ways Eva and Franklin have got it made. They could be very happy together and have a very happy family. To all intents and purposes in fact they have and this is something that is very much in the book that we wanted to retain. They are a good couple but they are keeping secrets, both from each other and from themselves. Eva's foot is on the brake and she can't bring herself to tell the truth. It's a very tough truth to tell and in many ways irrevocable. Once you have a child there are things you can't turn back.

JW: *What would you say about the film's treatment of grief? Eva seems to take the hatred that Kevin's act inspires upon herself.*

TS: She does because it's hers. When a complete stranger hits her in the face and somebody comes up to help her, Eva says 'it's my fault'. The red paint is hers to clean up. In many ways you could say that this is a consolation to her given that Kevin, the cause of all this violence has come out of her. He is absolutely enacting her misanthropy and her alienation and her violence. You could say that she really becomes a mother to Kevin once he is incarcerated. There is a moment in the book that we shot for the film but didn't include in the final cut, when Eva is visiting Kevin in prison and she asks him 'why didn't you kill me?' and Kevin responds, 'when you are putting on a show you don't kill the audience'. This really sheds light on Kevin's impetus and the pact that they have. It also makes clear his role as her nemesis. He's there to bring her to trial. And he does it and she does finally, and this may be sick to say, develop a purpose for the first time in her life and is actually focused.

JW: *Ezra Miller never tips over into a caricature of evil.*

TS: He is very impressive but it is important to note that he takes his lead from the equally impressive performance of Jasper Newell. Jasper sets the tone for Kevin for the majority of the story and what Ezra does is pick up the threads laid down by Jasper. I'm personally really interested in this element of the film because it's what we are dealing with, the subject of upbringing. It's not about a fifteen-year-old going and shooting up a school; it's about how do you bring up a child and how do you bring up a child of Jasper's age? The perpetration of all the things Eva is most ashamed of happened when Kevin was a toddler and so by the time Ezra comes along the damage has been done in terms of Eva's responsibility.

Ezra is certainly a tremendous asset to the film and we were very happy to have found him. We could have gone a number of different ways with the character of Kevin. In the book Lionel Shriver makes Kevin quite featureless. This is very interesting for a novel but almost impossible to affect in terms of cinema because you need to in some way inhabit the black hole that Kevin is in the book.

JW: *From Derek Jarman through to Lynn Hershman-Leeson, Sally Potter, Béla Tarr, Jim Jarmusch and Luca Guadagnino you have acquired a reputation as an artist who seeks out collaborators with distinct and unique visions. Is it important to you to remain inspired and challenged by the directors and material with which you work?*

TS: I honestly don't know how else to do it. It's a habit that I got right from the beginning from working with Derek and that's what I'm in it for. I'm not in it for anything else. No other game is worth the candle. You have to remember that I wasn't a trained performer and I have been very fortunate to go on and had these collaborators and forged these collaborations. They have kept me going this far. I tend to think of the collaborations as conversations and after what was a very fruitful, nine-year conversation with Derek Jarman I set myself a tough act to follow. I have been very fortunate to have these further conversations.

JW: *You have also used your increasing stature to act as a producer for films including* Thumbsucker *[2005] and* I Am Love *[2009]. Do you feel it's important to enable new voices in cinema to be heard?*

TS: To be honest with you this is what I have always done. To all intents and purposes I have co-produced. I certainly did it with Derek's films, and Sally Potter and I developed *Orlando* together over a period of five years. It's only in the last few years that it made sense to put my name out there publically. I'm not particularly interested in having my name put out there publically as a producer but it's just being honest about what I am doing, especially with something like *I Am Love* which was developed over a decade-long period. It's also interesting, of course, for the purposes of my bank manager so that he doesn't think that I am trying to pull the wool over his eyes when I ask to re-mortgage.

Wim **Wenders**

Born in Düsseldorf in 1945, Wim Wenders started taking photographs at the age of seven. He studied medicine and philosophy before settling in 1966 as a painter and engraver in Paris. In his spare time, he watched all the movies that were showing at the Cinémathèque, including many German classics. Soon after, he enrolled at the newly founded Film and Television Academy in Munich and went on to make several short films, which were influenced by the so-called 'New American Underground' – long scenes, uneventful and with an open narrative in the style of Warhol. His feature film debut was in 1970 with his graduation film, the black and white *Summer in the City*.

Wenders was one of the fifteen directors and writers who in 1971 founded the Filmverlag der Autoren to handle production, rights and distribution of their films. His professional career as a director began that year with the film adaptation of Peter Handke's novel *The Goalkeeper's Fear of the Penalty* (1972) for which he was awarded the International Film Critics Prize in Venice.

In *Alice in the Cities* (1973), *The Wrong Move* (1974) and *Kings of the Road* (1975) Wenders turns to characters who have to deal with their lack of roots in post-war Germany. These three films, as well as the thriller *The American Friend* (1977), an adaptation of Patricia Highsmith's *Ripley's Game* with Dennis Hopper and Bruno Ganz in the lead roles, grappled with the rapid change of his own country and established the director as one of the key figures of the New German Cinema. Rock and roll, drift and the affectionate curiosity of the observer to the world became the key facets of his work.

In 1978 Wenders was invited to the US by Francis Ford Coppola and began work for Zoetrope on the much troubled *Hammett* (1982). To ease the pain Wenders also shot and completed the Golden Lion-winning *The State of Things*, a sombre reflection on the art of filmmaking. *Paris, Texas* (1984) was a happier American sojourn.

A key road movie, the film was written by Sam Shepard, elevated Wenders to new international heights and won him the coveted Cannes Palme d'Or.

Berlin beckoned and the director duly returned to produce a city symphony-cum-fairytale, *Wings of Desire* (1987), in which an angel (played by Bruno Ganz) gives up immortality for the love of a woman. A sequel, *Faraway, So Close* followed in 1993. The globetrotting *Until the End of the World* (1990) ran over budget and its obvious ambition was thwarted by the truncated cut that was released. Wenders' career began to wobble. The intense and mysterious *The End of Violence* (1996) was followed by the generally disappointing *The Million Dollar Hotel* (1996).

The director's critical and commercial fortunes were revived by the multiple award-winning *The Buena Vista Social Club* (1999). A collaboration with regular cohort Ry Cooder, this documentary offered an intimate look at a group of veterans of the Cuban music scene. Wenders has often segued between fiction and documentary projects (most notably 1980's astonishing Nic Ray portrait *Lightning Over Water*) and after two somewhat lacklustre fiction features, *Don't Come Knocking* (2005) and the little seen *The Palermo Shooting* (2008), Wenders returned to factual filmmaking with *Pina* (2011). A portrait of the influential choreographer Pina Bausch that truly explored the possibilities of the 3D format, the film placed Wenders once more at the forefront of international cinema.

Something of a polymath, Wenders has also written several books on cinema and numerous books of photography. His artwork has also been exhibited worldwide.

The interview below took place to mark a major retrospective at the BFI Southbank in 2010.

JASON WOOD: *Your work rate suggests that you are not someone who likes to look back. However, on the occasion of this major retrospective what thoughts, memories and perceptions do you have regarding some of your past filmmaking endeavours?*

WIM WENDERS: There's a strange thing about looking back. Of course I dread the embarrassment that inevitably comes with it. There are always scenes and shots or even entire films that I regret or that I should have done otherwise, or would have wanted to do otherwise, if the limitations would have allowed me to. And then there are scenes and shots or entire films that I know I could never do again. I realise I wouldn't have that in me anymore. That is a very troubling feeling.

I'm not a very 'cerebral' filmmaker, I work mainly from the gut so when you see what once came out unconsciously, or without much reflection or at least without cautiousness, you start wondering who you were then and who you are now. And that concern I find pretty uncreative, sometimes plain scary. There's really nothing I fear more than to repeat myself. I try to avoid that as much as I consciously can. But going back in time and being confronted with my own work, I inevitably recognise just that: there are numerous subjects, themes, camera movements, framings, 'idiosyncrasies' and whatnot that reoccur and that pass through my work sometimes like subterranean connections. And I must say: I'd rather not know this stuff. I'd rather keep working under the assumption that I do things from scratch. Retrospectives tend to thrash this wishful thinking.

JW: *It's impossible to condense or distil your achievements but there is a sense that viewed collectively there are themes and concerns that recur: issues relating to communication; the road as a sense of both discovery and alienation, and the impact of the past. Do you see these as being subjects to which you are continually drawn, what continues to draw you to them and how has the way in which you have attempted to deal with these subjects changed?*

WW: When I was a young filmmaker and at the age of thirty had made six feature-length films, I noticed that many of my reviews, especially the English and American ones, summed up my work as dealing, basically, I quote. 'with Angst, America and Alienation'. I called these my 'triple-A reviews'. Undeniably, there was some truth in it. At least, I can say that in hindsight. Communication, the road, estrangement, and yes, the 'American colonialisation of our subconscious' were, and are, big subjects of my work. But while these themes continue to show up in my work, the points of view have changed. For a long time, my films were strictly seen through the eyes of my male heroes. But over the years women have played an increasingly important role and their absence is no longer a subject, like in *Alice in the Cities* or *Kings of the Road*. And, in very general terms, 'Love' has become an increasingly dominating subject. 'Places' also play a more important role, like Berlin, Tokyo, Lisbon or more recently Palermo. Plus there is an increased interest on my behalf in reality, even in political terms, so I have made a number of documentaries over the last few years.

JW: *From the moment you dedicated* Summer in the City *to* The Kinks *you have been inextricably linked to music and, perhaps, particularly rock and roll. Do you continue to draw inspiration from the art form and could you say something about the function music has played in your work?*

WW: My daily life is very much driven by music. I wake up with music, I write with music, I drive around with music. I have a great stereo system at home, and I love my iPod with my little 'Headroom' headphone amplifier on the road. I would not get on a plane without my music, for instance. I listen to a lot of new stuff every day, and I also cherish my 'old heroes'. So, in the development of a new film, either in the writing process or in the travelling and locations scouting period, there is always some music that imposes itself and that is of particular importance in my life at that time. And then, when I shoot the film or when I sit in the editing room, that music tends to impose itself, and I try to work it in, as a tribute or an homage to the role it played in conceiving that film. Rock and roll and Blues have continued to be constant companions, but I also listen a lot to African music these days, to Jazz and to Bach.

JW: *You've also demonstrated a remarkable responsibility with regard to fostering and encouraging emerging film talent. Perhaps the most notable incident is your dedication of prize money to Atom Egoyan many years ago. Do you feel that it is a responsibility of more established filmmakers to do this in order that cinema continues to evolve and accommodate new blood?*

WW: When I got interested in filmmaking, and finally totally immersed in it, the part that some of my 'father figures' played for me was invaluable. The advice I got from Sam Fuller, the friendship with Nicholas Ray, the telegram by François Truffaut, the inspiration of Yasujiro Ozu and Andrej Tarkovsky, learning from the films of John Ford and Anthony Mann, the contact with John Cassavetes, the call to come to America by Francis Coppola, you name it, that helped me more than any film school.

So I have always felt I had been given so much, I have received so much not only from individuals but also from the history of cinema. It was only natural, or totally evident, that I would have to give something back. I have been teaching for the last fifteen years, on a regular basis, and I was lucky that among my assistants and collaborators there have been such marvellous talents as Claire Denis and Allison Anders. And I was able to help emerging filmmakers like Jim Jarmusch, Chris Petit and Lucian Segura, among others. More recently there has been Holger Ernst and Robinson Savary.

JW: *You have entered another extremely creative and prolific period. What challenges still await you and in the years since you first set out what have been the most significant developments – technical or otherwise – in filmmaking?*

WW: When I made my first films, you had the choice between 16mm and 35mm, and between colour (expensive then) and black and white. Those were the only choices. When we mixed *The Goalkeeper's Fear of the Penalty* the process lasted one day. We had all the sounds of the film on four tracks and we mixed it straight to optical!

Today you have an almost infinite amount of choices of how you want to approach a film. You can turn big ideas into small-budget movies, and you can let your subject and your desire for freedom and independence tell you if you want to shoot on film, with an enlarged range of formats, or on digital, also with a whole variety of approaches. And sound is a whole other story. The greatest progress I witnessed was certainly the boost that soundscaping, moving from being strictly mono and optical, or magnetic, to digital stereo sound.

When I started out as a young director, limitations were rigorous. Your budget basically dictated what you were able to achieve, or to say. Today, thanks to digital technology, you can say a lot with very little means; unfortunately, the reverse is also true: if you have big means you're not allowed to say much anymore. You can be so much more spontaneous and flexible now. I am much more 'independent' today than I was able to be when I set out.

I feel it is a great privilege to work today, in the digital age, just as much as it has been a privilege to start at a time when you could still be in touch with the very beginning of filmmaking. I have worked with actors who began their career in silent movies! And I was able to still work with a cameraman in Henri Alekan who had been an assistant to a pioneer like Eugen Schüfftan!

Ben **Wheatley**

Brighton-based filmmaker Ben Wheatley is undoubtedly one of the most singular talents to emerge in recent British cinema. Incredibly productive and able to work within the confines of a minimal budget, Wheatley's work, made in collaboration with his partner Amy Jump, is characterised by its rippling undercurrent of menace and its distinctly off-kilter take on the British landscape.

Wheatley's debut, *Down Terrace* (2009), went largely unseen on release but has steadily grown in stature. Taking the best elements of *The Sopranos* and giving them a very British twist, the film focuses on the kind of issues faced by all families. Such as who grassed up son Karl (Robin Hill) to the local police? How will Dad Bill (Robert Hill) explain the recent profit drop to his bosses in London? Can Uncle Eric dispose of a body without making a mess of it again? And what should Mum Maggie (Julia Deakin) make for tea? When Bill suspects there's a mole in his criminal operation, he decides it's time to clean house and recrimination, betrayal, murder and a spot of redecorating are quick to follow. But as Bill and his family soon discover, you're only as good as the people you know. A very British crime drama laced with very black humour, *Down Terrace* also boasts incredibly inventive special effects, many of them executed by the director himself.

Kill List (2011) made more of an instant impression. Eight months after a disastrous job in Kiev left him physically and mentally scarred, ex-soldier turned contract killer, Jay (Neil Maskell), is pressured by his partner, Gal (Michael Smiley), into taking a new assignment. As they descend into the dark and disturbing world of the contract, Jay begins to unravel once again – his fear and paranoia sending him deep into the heart of darkness. Described by Wheatley as an attempt to make a genuinely scary horror film, *Kill List* really gets under the skin. Incredibly disturbing, there is a sense of foreboding from the very first frame and the film shines a light into some extremely dark and disturbed areas of the human psyche.

Sightseers (2012) is *Carry On Camping* for psychopaths. Ginger-bearded, caravanning enthusiast Chris (Steve Oram) wants to show his new girlfriend Tina (Alice Lowe) his world and he wants to do it his way; on a journey through the British Isles in his beloved caravan. Up until now Tina has led a sheltered life with her over-protective mother, but there are things that Chris wants her to see: the Crich Tramway Museum, the Ribblehead Viaduct, the Keswick Pencil Museum and the rolling countryside that accompanies these wonders in his life. But it doesn't take long for the dream to fade. Litterbugs, noisy teenagers and pre-booked caravan sites, not to mention Tina's meddling mother, soon conspire to shatter Chris's dreams and send him, and anyone who rubs him up the wrong way, over a very jagged edge…

Wheatley's most recent work is perhaps his finest. It's also his most disturbing. And that's saying something. *A Field In England* (2013) is set during the English Civil War. A small group of deserters flee from a raging battle through an overgrown field. They are captured by two men: O'Neil (Michael Smiley) and Cutler (Ryan Pope). O'Neil, an alchemist, forces the group to aid him in his search to find hidden treasure that he believes is buried in the field. Crossing a vast mushroom circle, which provides their first meal, the group quickly descend into a chaos of arguments, fighting and paranoia, and, as it becomes clear that the treasure might be something other than gold, they slowly become victim to the terrifying energies trapped inside the field.

A psychedelic trip into magic and madness, the film became the first ever UK film released simultaneously in cinemas, on DVD and Bluray, on Film4 and on VoD.

JASON WOOD: *As with* Down Terrace, Kill List *and* Sightseers, *you take a very unique view of Britain. You have an uncanny ability to make even its more mundane qualities seem strange and threatening.*

BEN WHEATLEY: I work with what I see from where I am. I think we all have unique views in that respect. I guess its in my nature, and all the rest of the cast and crew if I can speak for them, to have a bit of a bleak outlook. I'm finding that you spend a lot of time planning what's in your work but there are other meanings that slip in that reveal a lot about your character which you might never have considered or wanted to keep hidden.

JW: *This is your first period film. What challenges did this present given your relatively limited budget and what levels of research did yourself and Amy undertake into the period? Was authenticity key to you? You certainly know your sexual diseases…*

A Field In England, Ben Wheatley, 2013 (Rook Films)

BW: We researched the period but we are not historians. Authenticity was important; we came at the project from the point of view of wanting to do it justice. I appreciate that we may have made errors here and there but we approached the material with respect and didn't change things just to suit the story. The budget didn't really affect the filmmaking. The script and budget level were developed hand in hand. A field, costumes for the characters, a tent. There's not a lot else needed to tell this tale.

JW: *What factors influenced your decision to shoot in black and white?*

BW: Black and White is beautiful. Its about texture rather than chroma, about the lines in the actors faces rather than about the colour of the sky. And of course it's in the past. They didn't have colour film in the past.

JW: *You have previously said that you have always wanted to make a horror film because you find so few of them to be actually scary. What aspects of the genre, if any, did you particularly draw upon for* A Field in England? *Though not a straight horror as such, it reminded me of the work of Michael Reeves'* Witchfinder General *[1968].*

BW: We were thinking about *Culloden* [1964], *Winstanley* [1976] and *Onibaba* [1964] in the early stages of development for *A Field in England*. We weren't thinking specifically about genre really. I was happy when we started to shoot the end of the film that it seemed to be like a cowboy film and that Reece started to look like a refugee from a Jodorowsky movie.

I don't tend to wring my hands thinking about other films too much to be honest. If influences do come they come in from the edges and we notice afterwards. *Witchfinder General* is set in a similar period but I can't say it was a major influence. They wear similar hats.

JW: *The film sees you working again with Michael Smiley, who featured in* Down Terrace *and* Kill List. *His performance is full of menace and intrigue. As a natural performer did you allow him to contribute a great deal to the character or was his part very tightly scripted?*

BW: This is the first film that I have made that has had no improvisation in it. We shot the script and in the edit maybe dropped a handful of lines. Its the clearest script-to-screen experience I've had. Having said that, the performances were free in themselves. Working with a cast like this it's not really my job to tell them what to do … just to nudge them.

JW: *Obviously best known for his comic work and alliance with The League of Gentleman, Reece Sheersmith impresses in a more dramatic role.*

BW: I love the League of Gentlemen. I remember it took me a long time to realise that there was only three of them performing in it, Reece especially is very hard to spot. He inhabits each role so totally. Michael Smiley introduced him to me. They had both been in *Burke and Hare* [2010] together when *Down Terrace* was released. We had him in mind for something but we weren't quite sure what. Then Amy Jump wrote the Whitehead part specifically for him and we were away.

JW: *I am always impressed by the way that you blend the comic and the horrific.*

BW: I actually don't find it so hard, but then that probably says more about me than anything else. My attitude to violence on screen is generally to be true to it. Show emotion, show humour, show violence. Don't hide the audience from it.

Michael **Winterbottom**

Michael Winterbottom is one of the most prolific and productive directors at work anywhere in the world. If his work is characterised by anything, it is by the regularity with which it arrives; he has probably made another couple of films by the time you have read this interview, and his refusal to be pinned down by budget, subject or genre. That's not to suggest that Winterbottom's work is in any way slapdash or ill-thought, more that in a British filmmaking environment that can seem hostile to funding Winterbottom, and his producing partner Andrew Eaton, are able to make interesting work on a regular basis.

The directors credits include *Butterfly Kiss* (Official Competition, Berlin Film Festival, 1995); *Jude* (Director's Fortnight, Cannes Film Festival, 1996; Winner, Michael Powell Award, Edinburgh Iinternational Film Festival); *Welcome to Sarajevo* (Official Selection, Cannes Film Festival, 1998); *I Want You* (In Competition, Berlin Film Festival, 1998); *cf* (In Competition, Cannes Film Festival; Winne, Best British Film, British Independent Film Awards, 1999); *The Claim* (In Competition, Berlin Film Festival); *24 Hour Party People* (In Competition, Cannes Film Festival, 2002), *In This World* (Winner, Golden Bear, Berlin International Film Festival, 2003); *Code 46* (In Competition, Venice Film Festival, 2003); *9 Songs* (2004); *A Cock and Bull Story* (Toronto Film Festival, 2005); *Road to Guantanamo* (Silver Bear, Best Director, Berlin Film Festival, 2006); *A Mighty Heart* (Official Selection, Cannes Film Festival, 2007); *Genova* (Best Director, San Sebastian Film Festival, 2008); *The Shock Doctrine* (Sundance Film Festival, 2009); *The Killer Inside Me* (In Competition, Berlin Film Festival, 2010) and *The Trip* (Toronto Film Festival, 2010).

I have interviewed Winterbottom a number of times and he is obviously willing to discuss his work but a little uncomfortable with the process. The interview below took place on the eve of the release of *Trishna* (2012), an adaptation of Thomas Hardy's *Tess of the D'Ubervilles*. Relocated to present-day rural Rajasthan and the thriving metropolis of Mumbai, it's a classic tale of love and tragedy in which Trishna (Freida Pinto) meets a wealthy young British businessman, Jay Singh (Riz Ahmed), who has come to India to work in his father's hotel business. After an accident destroys her father's Jeep, Trishna goes to work for Jay, and they fall in love. But despite their feelings for each other, their relationship must remain a secret due to the conflicting pressures of a rural society which is changing rapidly as a result of industrialisation, urbanisation and, above all, education. Their problems seem to be solved when Jay takes Trishna to an exciting new world of dance, vibrant life and possibilities – Mumbai. But Trishna harbours a dark secret that threatens the very heart of their love affair, and inequality remains at the centre of their relationship which will lead her to question Jay's intentions towards her.

Winterbottom has since reunited with Steve Coogan for the Paul Raymond biopic *The Look of Love* (2013).

──────

JASON WOOD: *Am I right in saying that the idea for* Trishna *originally came to you when you were making* Code 46?

MICHAEL WINTERBOTTOM: Yes, On *Code 46* we shot for a few days in Rajasthan. On one of the recces we visited the desert outside Ossian. I was with some crew from Mumbai, and there was an incredible contrast between the life and attitude of the crew from Mumbai and the people of the village, whose lives were just beginning to be affected by the forces of mechanisation, urbanisation, industrialisation, and above all education. It was this that reminded me of Hardy and *Tess*. In his last two novels Hardy is describing a world where the stable life and culture of the village is being transformed by all these things. People losing their jobs on the farms due to mechanisation, people moving to the towns, the railways providing physical mobility and along with that education offering the prospect of social mobility.

Having shot *Jude* as a traditional period film I felt that it might be possible in some ways to more accurately capture Hardy's world by transposing the story to India. For example, when we filmed a steam train in *Jude* it seemed nostalgic and picturesque, whereas for Hardy it represented speed and modernity. So the mobile phones, Jeeps and jets and TV of *Trishna* were a much simpler way of showing the impact of modern technology on a culture that had been static and stable for hundreds of years.

Trishna is a character who has more education than her parents, who doesn't speak the local dialect like her parents, who feels slightly set apart from those she works with and can dream of a better life. Trishna's tragedy is that she has one foot in the fixed, old rural world, and one foot in the new, mobile, urban world.

JW: *Can I also ask about the changes that you decided to make to* Tess of the D'Urbervilles, *not only in terms of the relocation to rural Rajasthan and the thriving metropolis of Mumbai but in terms of introducing new themes, merging characters into one and the fact that in your version there is an abortion rather than the birth of a child that dies.*

MW: Although we were taking *Tess* as a starting point, the story obviously had to make sense in the world of Ossian where it is set. We spent a lot of time talking to people there about the story, and how it would make sense in their lives. Everyone we spoke with, all the drivers, the hotel workers, the hospital workers etc said that if a daughter got pregnant before they were married, the family would try to abort the child before anyone outside the family found out. So we shot that scene in a clinic with a doctor who works a lot with women from rural communities.

Also, in Hardy religion is a specific target. He attacks the Church for excluding Tess because she has a child out of wedlock. In our story it is more the culture of the family and the society in general that disapproves. In fact we open the film in the Temple in Ossian where dancing girls are celebrated in ornate carvings. Sensuality and pleasure are much more accepted in the Hindu and Jain religions than in Christianity.

Trishna deals with the world of tourism, high-end tourism, where rich Westerners can live out their postcolonial fantasies. So this is a theme that is not in Hardy. Jay is a rich Brit acting like an eighteenth-century prince or colonial ruler. Trishna is a worker in the hotel who is reduced to a servant or concubine. But tourism is a major industry in Rajasthan as in many places. Many of the actors in our film do actually work in hotels and the tourism industry. For them it provides work, a career and economic independence. I hope the film captures these contradictions.

Perhaps the biggest change with regard to story has nothing to do with setting it in India. It was combining two characters into one. In *Tess* there are Angel and Alec, the spiritual versus the sensual. I think most people are a combination of both. Having worked with Riz Ahmed before I thought he was capable of bringing out that complexity in Jay. He does fall in love with Trishna, but he is rich and young and wants immediate gratification. If he stood back, he would realise that the consequences for Trishna of what he does would be huge, whereas he, as a man, and as a rich man, can get away with whatever he likes.

Riz is a very intelligent actor. I think this is the first time he's really played a romantic lead, and he really stepped up to the mark. You have to be able to like Jay, and at the same time see his weaknesses and Riz does this brilliantly.

JW: *What is it about Hardy's work that appeals and what qualities make it suitable for the screen?*

MW: I love Hardy. I first read him when I was a teenager and I loved him then. He is a great storyteller. Both *Jude* and *Tess* are great love stories. He achieves something very particular. He gives you a very intimate portrait of his hero or heroine, but he also shows the bigger picture, how their lives are determined or at least affected by the way in which society is organised. He is much more radical than many people think. And he's more optimistic.

Hardy frequently moves away from Tess's individual story and puts it in context – how it would be for other people rather than Tess. I think that was one of the most important aspects of the filming for us – to be with Trishna and Jay, but then to see the other people, to see the family, or the city, or the workers in the field or the factory or the hotel. To provide a context for the story, to give some sense of the connections between Trishna's story and the world around her.

JW: *Did you go back and re-watch Polanski's take on the novel?*

MW: I did watch it again. I saw it when it first came out and I fell in love with Nastassja Kinski. Then I got a chance to work with her on *The Claim*, which was also based on a Hardy novel. This time I watched it with one of my daughters who thought it was beautiful but very slow!

JW: *Landscape also forms a key part of your work, most recently the beautiful Lake District in* The Trip. *How did you set about working with Marcel Zyskind to capture the colours and textures of Mumbai and Rajasthan and what kind of contrasts and contradictions did you want to emphasise?*

MW: Marcel has worked with me on over ten films now I think. We always take the same approach, which is to try and capture what is there. I remember the first thing I ever directed was a documentary on Ingmar Bergman and I met Sven Nykvist who talked about how he and Bergman would go to a location and watch it in all the different lights and then try and recreate that. We take the same approach, except we shoot everything on location. So it is a question of being in the right place at the right time. After that it is pretty simple.

JW: *You are probably tired of being told how prolific you are but having followed your career from the outset I find both your work rate and your ability to move between styles and genres quite unique. Is part of it a desire to keep the filmmaking process fresh and exciting for yourself?*

MW: It is just that it is more fun to be making a film than not. The boring and frustrating periods are when you are trying to persuade financiers to give you money. Once you are working on the detail of the film it is very satisfying. So why not make lots of films? And anyway, everyone used to make a lot of films. It is relatively recently that it has become fashionable to spend a lot of time resting between shoots.

Also from Wallflower Press:

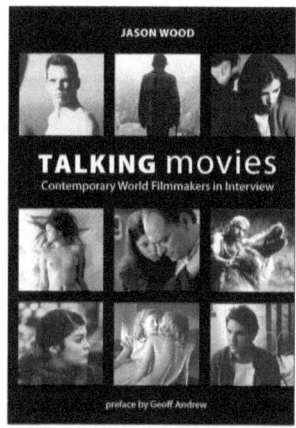

Talking Movies: Contemporary World Filmmakers in Interview
Jason Wood

Talking Movies is a collection of interviews with some of the most audacious and respected contemporary filmmakers of the present generation. Taken from over ten years of conversations for various films and publications, as well as numerous new unpublished interviews, directors selected for inclusion in this collection comprise figures whose work has defined how images are processed and appreciated by modern audiences. A truly international perspective is offered as the book includes numerous global pioneers; those frankly discussing their craft, and the social, political and technological forces that inform it, include Claire Denis, Laurent Cantet, Robert Guédiguian, Cédric Kahn, Lucile Hadzihalilovic and Bertrand Tavernier (France), John Sayles, David Gordon Green, Hal Hartley, Richard Linklater, Lodge Kerrigan, Bruce Weber and Scott McGehee & David Siegal (USA), Alejandro González Iñárritu, Guillermo del Toro and Carlos Reygadas (Mexico), Nicolas Roeg, Stephen Frears, Pawel Pawlikowski, Andrew Kötting, Asif Kapadia and Kim Longinotto (UK), Nuri Bilge Ceylan (Turkey), Atom Egoyan (Canada), Jan Švankmajer (Czech Republic), Suzanne Bier (Denmark), John Hillcoat & Nick Cave (Australia), Tranh Anh Hung (Vietnam), Samira Makhmalbaf (Iran), Elia Suleiman (Palestine) and Lucrecia Martel (Argentina). This volume is thus an indispensable insight into contemporary global cinema.

> 'This is no self-celebrating souvenir of glamorous meetings with particularly well-known men and women; it's a collection of unembellished transcriptions of informed, intelligent, down-to-earth conversations with hard-working filmmakers about the creative decisions they made, why they made them, and what the consequences of those decisions were. In each case, you get a real sense of people talking movies – actually thinking about cinema, rather than simply requiring and providing the usual trite soundbites.'
> – FROM THE PREFACE BY GEOFF ANDREW

JASON WOOD is a film programmer, documentary filmmaker and writer. He is the author of 100 American Independent Films (2004), Nick Broomfield: Documenting Icons (2005) and The Faber Book of Mexican Cinema (2006). His journalism has appeared in Vertigo, the Guardian and Sight and Sound.

224 pages
ISBN: 978-1-904764-90-8 (paperback)
ISBN: 978-1-904764-91-5 (cloth)

GPSR Authorized Representative: Easy Access System Europe, Mustamäe tee 50, 10621 Tallinn, Estonia, gpsr.requests@easproject.com